# IN 100 SCENES

Written by DANIEL LIPKOWITZ

# A LONG TIME AGO....

Welcome to the story (so far) of LEGO®
*Star Wars*™. One hundred brick-built
scenes full of action, intrigue, betrayal,
more action, battles, droids, a smattering
of politics, heroes, an extra bit of action
– and a whole lot of surprises. Who
knew Han Solo would delve into the
intricacies of the Ewok language?
Who would have guessed Yoda's
favourite food was mud and bug
soup? For fun facts and more
incredible revelations, read on...

IF YOU'RE NOT CAREFUL, I MIGHT FIRE MY BLASTER.

HA! NOT IF I FIRE FIRST...

**DK** | Penguin
Random
House

**Project Editor** Shari Last
**Designers** Jon Hall and
Sam Bartlett
**Senior Pre-Production Producer** Jennifer Murray
**Senior Producer** Lloyd Robertson
**Managing Editor** Simon Hugo
**Design Manager** Guy Harvey
**Art Director** Lisa Lanzarini
**Publisher** Julie Ferris
**Publishing Director** Simon Beecroft

LEGO facts compiled by Christopher Pearce

Additional photography by Gary Ombler

DK would like to thank Randi Sørensen, Robert Stefan Ekblom,
Paul Hansford and Heike Bornhausen at the LEGO Group; J.W. Rinzler and
Leland Chee at Lucasfilm; and Tori Kosara at DK for editorial assistance.

First published in Great Britain in 2015
by Dorling Kindersley Limited
80 Strand, London WC2R ORL

Copyright © 2015 Dorling Kindersley Limited
A Penguin Random House Company
10 9 8 7 6 5 4 3 2 1
001–276631–Apr/15

A CIP catalogue record for this book
is available from the British Library.
ISBN: 978-0-24118-942-9

Colour reproduction in the UK by Altaimage Ltd, UK
Printed and bound in China

www.dk.com
www.LEGO.com/starwars

A WORLD OF IDEAS:
SEE ALL THERE IS TO KNOW

# CONTENTS

# EPISODE I

## THE PHANTOM MENACE

*Turmoil has engulfed the Galactic Republic.*

*The greedy Trade Federation has stopped all supplies reaching the small planet of Naboo, which is causing all kinds of problems.*

*The Supreme Chancellor of the Republic has sent two Jedi Knights to do their "peace and justice" thing.....*

# A JEDI MISSION

The Trade Federation has surrounded the planet of Naboo with its battleships, and refuses to let anyone pass. The Chancellor of the Republic sends two Jedi Knights, Qui-Gon Jinn and Obi-Wan Kenobi, to negotiate for peace. As their Republic cruiser nears Naboo, the Jedi prepare for the mission.

**RADIANT VII**
*Consular*-class Republic cruiser that transports Jedi negotiators and other diplomats around the galaxy.

**NABOO**
A tranquil world near the Outer Rim, home to the Naboo and Gungan peoples.

## REPUBLIC CRUISER

 Along with this LEGO Republic Cruiser from Episode I, there is a similar, more heavily-armed Republic Frigate set from the Clone Wars.

The Republic Cruiser appears in the 2005 LEGO® *Star Wars*™ video game.

# BATTLE DROID AMBUSH

Jedi Master Qui-Gon Jinn and his Padawan apprentice, Obi-Wan Kenobi, arrive on the Trade Federation flagship. But the leaders of the Federation are secretly working with the Sith Lord Darth Sidious, a powerful master of the dark side of the Force. Sidious orders them to destroy the Jedi.

## BATTLE DROIDS

 Battle droids are everywhere! They appear in 33 LEGO sets – more than any other minifigure. Roger roger.

 They might be called minifigures, but LEGO battle droids don't contain any standard minifigure parts.

**BATTLE DROID**
Mass-produced mechanical soldiers belonging to the Trade Federation. Obedient and dim-witted. Highly vulnerable to lightsabers. Easily replaced.

FIRST POISON GAS, AND NOW BATTLE DROIDS.

**OBI-WAN KENOBI**
Jedi apprentice to Qui-Gon Jinn. A skilled swordsman and Force wielder.

8

**DIOXIS GAS**
A toxic gas utilised by the Trade Federation for sneak attacks. It doesn't work so well on Jedi Knights.

"Oh dear, battle droids! Always 'Roger roger' this and 'Roger roger' that. If you ask me, a droid should never resort to violence. They certainly weren't very friendly... nor very bright."

CAN'T THE TRADE FEDERATION JUST ATTACK US IN PERSON?

THAT'S WHAT WE WANNA KNOW! HELP!!

SSSSSSSSSSS

**QUI-GON JINN**
Jedi Master. A kind and wise believer in the philosophy of the Living Force.

# ROYAL RESCUE

Qui-Gon and Obi-Wan escape to Naboo, but discover that the Trade Federation has already launched an invasion. With the help of the bumbling Gungan Jar Jar Binks, the Jedi set off aboard a Gungan submarine to rescue the planet's young queen, Padmé Amidala. If they can find her...

**PLANETARY CORE**
The tunnel-filled deep-sea centre of Naboo. A handy shortcut for Jedi in a hurry.

**TRIBUBBLE BONGO**
A bio-engineered Gungan submersible grown around a coral-like framework. Propelled by tentacle-like tail fins.

## GUNGAN SUB

 The Gungan Sub can split into smaller mini subs – a function that does not appear in the film.

 There have been two LEGO Gungan subs. In the earlier model, each minifigure had his own compartment.

**FISH**
There's always a bigger one.

"That Jar Jar was always getting himself into trouble, and the rest of us as well. Who would have ever believed at the time that he would end up becoming an official Republic Representative? Actually, I still don't believe it."

IT'S SO AWESOME MEETING SUCH NICE NEW PEOPLE! I FEEL THAT WEESA GOING TO BE THE BEST OF BESTEST FRIENDS.

MEESA SO HAPPY TO BE MAKING SO MANY BOMBAD NEW FRIENDS!

I WONDER IF I COULD SWIM BACK HOME FROM HERE...

JAR JAR BINKS
An accident-prone amphibious Gungan, exiled from the underwater city of Otoh Gunga for crashing ruler Boss Nass's heyblibber.

# DETOUR TO TATOOINE

After escaping from Naboo aboard Queen Amidala's royal starship, the fugitives have to make an emergency landing on the desert world of Tatooine after the ship is damaged. Qui-Gon, Padmé and Jar Jar go to look for a new hyperdrive generator, but they cannot pay the price demanded by Watto, the junk shop owner.

## WATTO

 Watto's head, chest piece and wings are on a single piece that covers most of his blue torso.

 The earlier version of Watto's minifigure was completely blue, with no printed details.

**WATTO'S SHOP**
A cluttered junk shop in the Tatooine city of Mos Espa.

**GNK DROID**
Watto's junk shop is littered with derelict droids.

HOW COME NOTHING EXCITING EVER HAPPENS ON TATOOINE?

**ANAKIN SKYWALKER**
Young slave boy owned by Watto. Affectionately known as "Ani".

**JUNK**
A random mix of mechanical components and spare parts. Useful for repairs if you can find – and afford – what you're looking for.

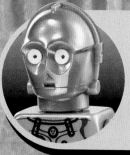

WHAT, YOU THINK YOU'RE SOME KIND OF JEDI, WITH YOUR JEDI MIND TRICKS AND JEDI ROBE AND JEDI LIGHTSABER? SAY, WAIT A MINUTE...

FLAP

FLAP

FLAP

**WATTO**
A Toydarian junk merchant. Gruff and selfish, but not completely bad. Immune to Jedi mind tricks. Doesn't take Republic credits.

# RACING FOR FREEDOM

Watto has a young slave called Anakin Skywalker who is a very skilled pilot. Qui-Gon senses the power of the Force in the boy and arranges for him to compete in a podrace. Anakin wins, acquiring the part the Jedi need and earning his freedom – though he has to leave behind his mother and C-3PO, the protocol droid he has built.

HEY, YOU'RE CHEATING!

**ANAKIN SKYWALKER**
A nine-year-old slave who is an excellent engineer and pilot despite his age. Incredibly strong in the Force, but completely untrained.

OF COURSE I'M CHEATING! I'M THE BAD GUY. HOW ELSE AM I SUPPOSED TO WIN?

**SEBULBA**
A member of the Dug species and champion of the Galactic Racing Circuit. His opponents have a strange habit of crashing in mid-race.

# PODRACERS

Two LEGO models of Sebulba's podracer have been produced. Both contain some of the devious Dug's hidden weaponry, including extendable buzz saws and a highly illegal flame thrower.

**ANAKIN'S PODRACER**
A custom-built repulsorlift racing vehicle assembled by Anakin. The small cockpit is pulled at high speeds by two Radon-Ulzer 620c turbine engines linked with plasma power couplings.

**SEBULBA'S PODRACER**
This custom-built podracer is powered by two Collar Pondrat Plug-F Mammoth Split-X engines and fuelled with illegally upgraded Tradium fuel – of course.

# THE SITH STRIKE

On their way back to the royal starship, a mysterious Sith warrior launches an attack. Darth Maul has been sent by his Master, Darth Sidious, to eliminate the Jedi and capture the queen. Qui-Gon holds him off with his lightsaber, and the heroes manage to get away.

> WHO ARE YOU?! WHAT DO YOU WANT?

## SITH INFILTRATOR

 The hull of the LEGO Sith Infiltrator is big enough to hold Maul's speeder and the probe droids. A working hatch allows them to be deployed.

 This is the third Sith Infiltrator model to have been released.

**TATOO I AND TATOO II**
The blazing twin suns of the Tatooine system.

"Oh dear, it's Darth Maul! If you don't mind, I'm going to go and hide for a little while. I wasn't around for this part of the story, anyway."

**PROBE DROID**
DRK-1 probe droid. Used by the Sith to track down enemies.

SORRY, BUT I'VE ONLY GOT TWO LINES IN THIS MOVIE — AND I'M NOT WASTING THEM NOW!

**THE *BLOODFIN***
Darth Maul's Sith vehicle, a modified Razalon FC-20 speeder bike. Weaponless, but extremely fast and manoeuvrable.

**DARTH MAUL**
A horned and tattooed Zabrak from the planet Dathomir. The first Sith seen in the galaxy in a thousand years. A relentless and almost unbeatable warrior.

# THE JEDI COUNCIL

Qui-Gon brings Anakin to the Jedi Temple on the Republic capital world of Coruscant. He believes that the boy is the Chosen One, destined to bring balance to the Force. But Jedi Master Yoda will not let Anakin be trained, saying that he is too old and too afraid to become a Padawan.

HE MIGHT BE LITTLE, BUT HE LOOKS LIKE MILLIGRAMS OF TROUBLE!

AW! A LITTLE YOUNGLING.

**JEDI HIGH COUNCIL**
A group of 12 revered Jedi Masters who guide the Jedi Order in its most important decisions and actions.

## JEDI COUNCIL

 The Jedi Council chamber has appeared in three *Star Wars* movies, but never in a LEGO set.

 Nevertheless, six of the 12 Jedi Council members from Episode I have appeared in minifigure form.

# GUNGAN ALLIES

Despite lots of advice from the helpful Senator Palpatine, Padmé Amidala cannot convince the Senate to help defend the planet Naboo from the invading Trade Federation. Together with her new friends, Padmé prepares to fight the Trade Federation. Fortunately, they are able to convince the Gungans to join them in battle.

## ON THE BATTLEFIELD

 The LEGO Troop Carrier vehicle released in 2011 can carry eight folded battle droids, plus two pilots.

 A total of eight LEGO sets depict the events of the Battle of the Great Grass Plains.

**BATTLE OF THE GREAT GRASS PLAINS**
While Queen Amidala and the Jedi sneak into the capital city of Theed, the Gungans keep the Trade Federation's droid forces occupied outside the city.

**MULTI-TROOP TRANSPORT**
Each of these repulsorlift vehicles can transport 112 droids to the battlefield.

WEESA BE MESSEN UP ALLA THESE MACHINEEKS WITH OUR BOOMAS, BOYOS!

**TRADE FEDERATION TROOP CARRIER**
Hovering repulsorlift vehicles that carry battle droids into combat, folded up for convenient transport in their storage racks.

**PILOT BATTLE DROID**
A battle droid with special programming for driving and piloting vehicles. Identifiable by its blue body markings.

66 Hello! Just in case you aren't fluent in six million forms of communication (like I am), then what Jar Jar just said was, 'We are annihilating the Trade Federation's battle droid army with our plasma energy spheres, my fine fellow Gungans!' More or less, anyway. 99

# DARTH MAUL RETURNS

In a hangar bay near the Theed Royal Palace, the heroes encounter Darth Maul once more. As Qui-Gon and Obi-Wan draw their lightsabers and face him, Padmé plans to capture the leaders of the Trade Federation. Anakin hides inside a parked starfighter, but is trapped when it automatically launches into space.

**THEED HANGAR**
Headquarters of the Royal Naboo Security Forces. Currently under attack.

**NABOO FIGHTER PILOT**
Elite soldier from the Naboo Royal Navy. Trained to pilot N-1 starfighters.

**SECURITY BATTLE DROID**
A slightly advanced version of the regular battle droid, programmed to detect security risks. Clearly, they are not always successful.

ROGER ROGER.

STOP CALLING ME ROGER!

PNNKK

The LEGO Flash Speeder set (7124) is the only set that represents the Theed Palace battle.

A miniature LEGO model of the planet Naboo was produced in 2012 as part of the Planets series.

"Thank the Maker I wasn't present during this battle! An actual Sith Lord, goodness me. I would have quite short circuited! Master Ani was much braver than I – though I must say, hiding inside a starfighter was an excellent idea. Best to keep out of the way."

**DOUBLE-BLADED LIGHTSABER**
Darth Maul's saberstaff can extend red lightsaber blades from both of its ends, letting him duel against two Jedi at the same time.

WE'LL HOLD HIM OFF WHILE YOU RUN!

**CAPTAIN PANAKA**
Leader of the Royal Naboo Security Forces, and responsible for ensuring the queen's safety.

YIKES! YOU DON'T HAVE TO TELL US TWICE!

**QUEEN AMIDALA**
Padmé Naberrie Amidala is the democratically elected ruler of Naboo. She is clever, brave and dedicated to protecting her people.

# A MATTER OF TIMING

The two Jedi and the Sith wage a furious and acrobatic duel that leads them through a generator complex, where a force field suddenly separates Obi-Wan from the others. He can only watch helplessly as Darth Maul strikes Qui-Gon a fatal blow with his lightsaber.

**HELPLESS PADAWAN**
Young Obi-Wan watches in horror as his Master is attacked.

I'LL BET YOU WISH YOU HAD AN EXTRA LIGHTSABER BLADE NOW, TOO.

**CRIMSON BLADES**
Darth Maul fashioned the crystals for his lightsaber himself, using meditation, a compression chamber and the Force.

**LASER GATE**
One of a series of impenetrable, lightsaber-proof energy barriers that protect the complex's exhaust shaft. Each gate is deactivated for only seconds at a time.

**QUI-GON JINN**

Qui-Gon's hair piece was exclusive to him until 2013, when it appeared in the LEGO® *Hobbit*™ theme.

In some of the 2007 Republic Cruiser sets Qui-Gon accidentally came with Obi-Wan's head!

MOSTLY I WISH I HAD WAITED FOR OBI-WAN TO GET HERE...

**PLASMA REFINERY COMPLEX**
A large building next to the Royal Palace of Theed on Naboo, where valuable plasma is extracted from the planet's core to power the city and for export off-world.

## DARTH MAUL

▶ Darth Maul might have a double-bladed lightsaber, but its hilt is the same as any other LEGO lightsaber.

▶ There are six Zabrak minifigures: Maul, Savage Opress, Agen Kolar, Eeth Koth, Sugi and Old Republic Jedi Knight.

# THE FALL OF MAUL

When the force field vanishes, Obi-Wan leaps to confront the Sith who has slain his Master. Darth Maul is sure he can defeat the inexperienced Jedi, but his overconfidence is his downfall. Obi-Wan's talent with the Force enables him to deliver justice for Qui-Gon and end the peril of Darth Maul.

**WITHOUT A MASTER**
Now a Padawan with no Master, Obi-Wan will soon be named a Knight by the Jedi Council and given a Padawan of his own — young Anakin Skywalker.

# THE BATTLE OVER NABOO

Somehow, Anakin finds himself in the middle of a space battle high above Naboo. With his podracer piloting skills, some help from R2-D2 and a little luck, he outflies the Trade Federation's droid starfighters and blows up the ship that is controlling their droid soldiers on the ground below.

**DROID CONTROL SHIP**
A Trade Federation warship that remotely commands and coordinates entire battle droid armies. Without its signals, the droids shut down.

**TRADE FEDERATION VULTURE DROID**
Attack starfighter with an internal droid brain. Can convert to a walking mode that uses its wings as legs.

THE CHILD PILOT IS GETTING AWAY! FIRE! *FIRE!*

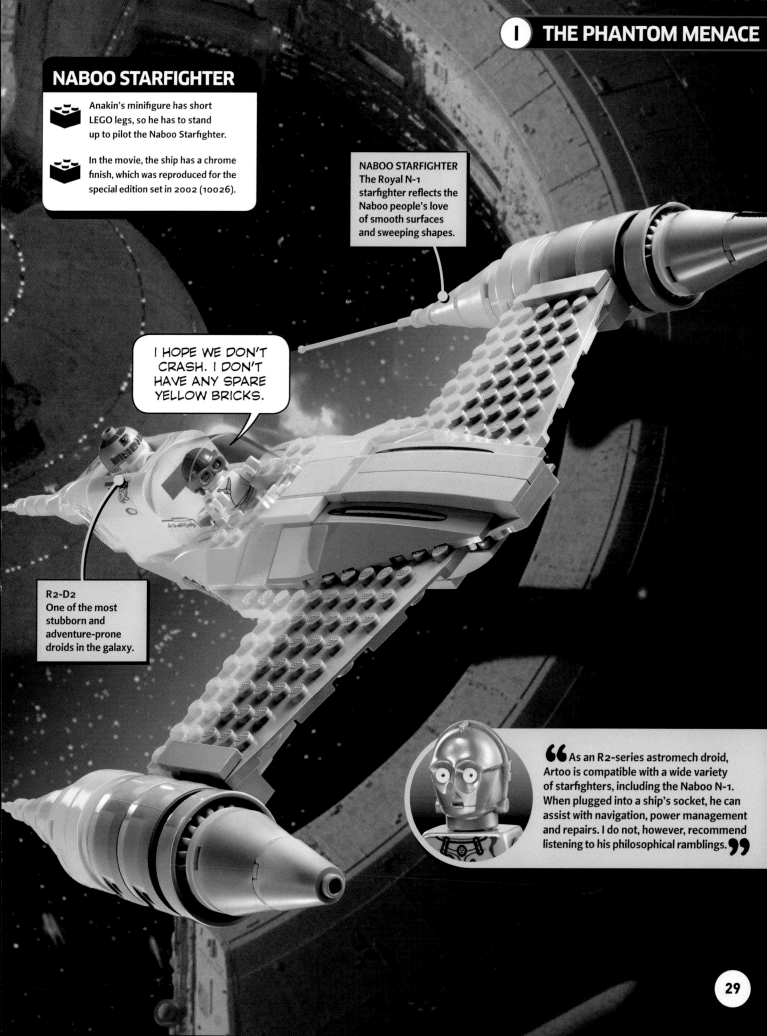

## NABOO STARFIGHTER

Anakin's minifigure has short LEGO legs, so he has to stand up to pilot the Naboo Starfighter.

In the movie, the ship has a chrome finish, which was reproduced for the special edition set in 2002 (10026).

**NABOO STARFIGHTER**
The Royal N-1 starfighter reflects the Naboo people's love of smooth surfaces and sweeping shapes.

I HOPE WE DON'T CRASH. I DON'T HAVE ANY SPARE YELLOW BRICKS.

**R2-D2**
One of the most stubborn and adventure-prone droids in the galaxy.

❝As an R2-series astromech droid, Artoo is compatible with a wide variety of starfighters, including the Naboo N-1. When plugged into a ship's socket, he can assist with navigation, power management and repairs. I do not, however, recommend listening to his philosophical ramblings.❞

29

# HAPPY ENDING

With the droid army deactivated, the Trade Federation defeated and the Sith apparently destroyed, Naboo is free again. Palpatine becomes the new Supreme Chancellor of the Republic and Obi-Wan is allowed to train Anakin as a Jedi. There is a grand celebration... but the dark side's schemes have only just begun.

**GUNGAN SOLDIER**
Members of the Gungan Grand Army, called "Militiagungs". Armed with plasma-ball throwing sticks and personal energy shields.

**CHANCELLOR PALPATINE**
A senator from Naboo, now the newly elected Supreme Chancellor. A very influential man.

> SO WHAT WAS THE PHANTOM MENACE, ANYWAY?

> BEEP BLEEOOP!

GENERAL JAR JAR BINKS
The clumsy Gungan has successfully been promoted to the rank of general.

WHO CARES? WE'RE HAVING A PARTY!

PALACE STEPS
A victory parade through the streets of Naboo leads to the palace steps.

## VICTORY PARADE

Minifigures do not appear in the celebration outfits they wear during the final scene of the movie.

Since 1999, 29 sets depicting the events of Episode I have been released by the LEGO Group.

31

# EPISODE II

## ATTACK OF THE CLONES

*The stable Republic is being threatened by the Separatists — an imaginatively named group who want to separate from the Republic, which might mean a war.*

Senator Amidala (did she get demoted from Queen?) *is* attending a Senate vote on establishing a Republic army. Sounds like a good idea — perhaps someone should have thought of this a while ago!

Meanwhile, the Jedi are still being heroes....

# A SENATOR IN DANGER

Ten years have passed since the Battle of Naboo, and Anakin has grown into a gifted but reckless Jedi Padawan under Obi-Wan's teaching. When a shape-shifting assassin tries to dispatch Padmé, now a Republic senator, Obi-Wan and Anakin chase the criminal through the skyscrapers of Coruscant. Before they can capture her, the assassin is poisoned by a mysterious attacker.

**TRAFFIC**
On Coruscant, it isn't just in front of and behind you – it's above and below you, too.

**ZAM WESELL**
A Clawdite bounty hunter who can change her natural reptilian appearance to mimic other humanoid life forms.

***KORO*-2 EXODRIVE AIRSPEEDER**
Zam Wesell's fork-nosed speeder. Powered by an electromagnetic field generated around its forward mandibles.

THIS SPEEDER IS SO COOL!

**XJ-6 AIRSPEEDER**
One-of-a-kind twin-turbofan speeder, owned by a Republic senator until commandeered by Anakin Skywalker.

UH, RIGHT. ARE YOU EVEN OLD ENOUGH TO DRIVE, ANAKIN?

**CORUSCANT CHASE**

The headlights on Anakin's commandeered airspeeder are actually silver LEGO cup pieces.

Shape-shifter Zam Wesell was the first LEGO® *Star Wars*™ minifigure to have a double-sided head.

**SKYSCRAPER**
The city world of Coruscant is famous for its skyscrapers, which dwarf the mountains and other natural features of the planet.

# CLONE ARMY

While Anakin and Padmé travel undercover to ensure Padmé's safety, Obi-Wan tracks the shadowy attacker from Coruscant to the planet Kamino. There, Obi-Wan is surprised to find a facility full of clone troopers. He is told that they have been manufactured as an army for the Jedi.

**CLONE TROOPER**
One of an identical army of Republic troopers created and trained in the cloning facilities of Kamino.

YEP, WE'RE ALL EXACTLY THE SAME.

## CLONE TROOPERS

They might be clones, but the head piece beneath the helmet varies from one minifigure to the next. Some clone troopers have all black head pieces, while others are printed with a surly expression or a piercing stare.

"Ah yes, Kamino. I recall hearing about how surprised everybody was to learn of a secret clone army being built for the Jedi. It did seem awfully suspicious, but it is not my place to voice personal opinions."

I'M NOT!

HUSH, 1132.

CC-1137
A clone.

CC-1139
Also a clone.

CLONE TROOPER PHASE I ARMOUR
A protective layer of plastoid-alloy composite plates over a black bodysuit. One size fits all clones.

37

# BOUNTY HUNTER

The troopers have been cloned from an accomplished bounty hunter by the name of Jango Fett. Obi-Wan suspects that Fett is the one he is looking for – and he's right. Obi-Wan and Jango have a duel on a Kamino landing pad, but the bounty hunter escapes on his starship with his young son and clone, Boba.

## JANGO FETT

A Santa version of Jango Fett's minifigure was released in the 2013 LEGO *Star Wars* Advent Calendar. This jolly Jango carries gifts in his utility belt, is decorated with holly and has a frilly white printed collar.

YOU WON'T GET AWAY, BOUNTY HUNTER!

**LANDING PAD**
May be slippery when wet... and it's almost always raining on Kamino.

# DOGFIGHT IN SPACE

Obi-Wan uses a homing beacon to follow Jango's ship, *Slave I*, to the rocky world of Geonosis. When Jango attacks Obi-Wan's starfighter in an asteroid field, however, the Jedi is outmatched by an arsenal of hidden weapons. Obi-Wan is forced to fake his own ship's destruction to survive.

## SLAVE I

 Eleven LEGO models of *Slave I* have been released, including six sets and five mini models.

 Of the eleven, only three are flown by Jango. The other eight feature grown-up Boba as the pilot.

THIS IS JUST AS BAD AS FLYING DURING RUSH HOUR ON CORUSCANT.

**OBI-WAN'S JEDI STARFIGHTER**
Delta-7 *Aethersprite*-class light interceptor. Red and white colouration represents the Jedi Order's diplomatic immunity – not that a bounty hunter is likely to care.

**R4-P17**
Integrated astromech droid navigator.

JUST ANOTHER WORK DAY, ROCKIN' OUT IN AN ASTEROID FIELD.

**SLAVE I**
A *Firespray-31*-class patrol and attack starship. Originally a police vessel, but customised by Jango Fett for his work.

**GEONOSIS**
Barren, rocky landscape is home to great hive colonies of the Geonosians.

**ASTEROID BELT**
The route to Geonosis is obstructed by thousands of asteroids.

# ANAKIN'S RAGE

Returning to Tatooine, Anakin learns that his mother has been kidnapped by Tusken Raiders. When he is too late to save her, he takes a terrible revenge on the entire Tusken camp. Soon afterwards, he and Padmé receive a message from Geonosis and learn that Obi-Wan has been captured.

## TUSKEN RAIDERS

 Tusken Raiders make an appearance in three *Star Wars* movies – but in just two LEGO sets.

 The Tusken Raider minifigure has also appeared in every LEGO *Star Wars* video game to date.

GADERFFII
A spike-tipped club, the traditional weapon of the Tusken Raiders. Also called a gaffi stick.

# ENTER COUNT DOOKU

On the planet Geonosis, Obi-Wan has discovered a Separatist plot to attack the Republic. The Separatists are led by Count Dooku – a former Jedi Master and now the Sith Lord Darth Tyranus. Dooku tries to convince Obi-Wan to join them, but the Jedi refuses. When Anakin and Padmé arrive to rescue Obi-Wan, they are caught too.

## COUNT DOOKU

 Count Dooku can count three LEGO minifigures of himself. Over the years, his face has grown progressively meaner, and his facial hair has become increasingly detailed.

COUNT DOOKU
Leader of the Separatists, Count Dooku is an arrogant Sith Lord. He left the Jedi Order and joined the dark side as Darth Sidious's second apprentice.

SO YOU SEE, WE'RE ACTUALLY BEING TOTALLY REASONABLE BY WANTING TO DESTROY THE REPUBLIC.

YES, I CAN SEE HOW REASONABLE YOU'RE BEING — BY THE WAY YOU'VE IMPRISONED ME IN THIS FLOATING FORCE FIELD!

**GEONOSIAN HIVE**
An underground network of tunnels created by the insectoid Geonosians.

**CONTAINMENT FIELD**
Geonosian device that suspends prisoners in midair. It disrupts concentration, and blocks use of the Force.

# GEONOSIS ARENA

Obi-Wan, Anakin and Padmé are sentenced to be executed in the Geonosis arena, where they must fight ferocious beasts and bug-like Geonosians. Just when they are about to be blasted by destroyer droids, help arrives in the form of Jedi Master Mace Windu, leading a Jedi rescue team.

## SUPER BATTLE DROID

LEGO super battle droids come in two colours: metallic pearl blue and metallic dark grey.

The most recent variant of the super battle droid minifigure has a built-in blaster on its left forearm.

**DESTROYER DROID**
"Droideka" assault droid. Deploys in wheel form and then unfolds to fight while protected by a deflector shield.

❝Due to a mishap in a Geonosian factory, I ended up with my head on top of a battle droid's body, and a battle droid's head on mine! It was all rather confusing until Artoo managed to straighten things out.❞

**GEONOSIAN WARRIOR**
Winged, flying members of the Geonosian warrior caste. They attack in large numbers with sonic cannons.

**SUPER BATTLE DROID**
Enhanced battle droid model with upgraded armour and built-in arm laser cannons.

DID SOMEONE CALL FOR A BUNCH OF *AWESOME* JEDI MASTERS?

NUH-UH.

IT WASN'T US!

# MACE VS. JANGO

As the rest of the Jedi battle the Geonosians and Separatist battle droids, Mace Windu faces off against Jango Fett on the dusty floor of the arena. Both opponents are highly skilled, but only one has the power of the Force on his side. Soon it is all over. Jango Fett falls, defeated by his Jedi foe.

## THE FETTS

 The Boba Fett minifigure pictured here is exclusive to the 2013 LEGO *Star Wars* Advent Calendar.

 When Boba grows up, his minifigure reflects his respect for his dad. Boba's armour is based on Jango's.

**BOBA FETT**
Jango's young son. As his clone, he takes after his father in every way. The seeds of vengeance are about to be sown.

LISTEN UP, BOBA. RULE NUMBER ONE DURING A FIGHT: KEEP CALM – DON'T LOSE YOUR HEAD.

**MANDALORIAN ARMOUR**
Human Jango was adopted by the warriors of Mandalore as a child. He grew up to become one of them and proudly wore their traditional armour.

**MACE'S LIGHTSABER**
A unique purple-bladed weapon constructed with a violet lightsaber crystal.

GOOD ADVICE, JANGO. IT GIVES ME AN IDEA...

**MACE WINDU**
A powerful, strong-willed Jedi Master and member of the Jedi High Council. Few can stand against his formidable lightsaber technique and Force abilities.

**COLEMAN TREBOR**
Jedi Council member. Known for his diplomatic skills, though they're not of much use right now.

# HERE COMES THE CAVALRY

Despite Mace's victory, the Jedi are still hopelessly outnumbered by the Separatist droids. All seems lost until an unexpected but welcome green face appears to even the odds. Master Yoda has come, and he has brought the entire clone trooper army with him.

**REPUBLIC GUNSHIP**
Clone trooper carriers, called Low Altitude Assault Transports (LAATs). Independent ion repeater turrets prevent the engines from overheating.

JUST POINT US AT THE BAD GUYS, SIR.

HERE TO SAVE THE DAY WE ARE!

**GRAND ARMY OF THE REPUBLIC**
The Republic's army of clone troopers. Led by Jedi Generals, but ultimately loyal to the Supreme Chancellor. Good thing they're all on the same side.

## REPUBLIC GUNSHIP

Three LEGO Republic gunships have been produced over the years. Each is larger than its predecessor.

There are two cockpits on the 2013 Republic gunship – but only one pilot!

# THE COUNT FLEES

With the tide of battle turning, Count Dooku decides that survival is more important than gloating. He hops onto his speeder and flies to his secret hangar, planning to depart Geonosis with the designs for an ultimate weapon. But Anakin and Obi-Wan do not intend to let him leave so easily.

**GEONOSIAN STARFIGHTER**
*Nantex*-class territorial defence starfighter. Geonosian starships that service and assist the Separatist army on Geonosis.

I'M NOT RUNNING AWAY. I'M ADVANCING VERY QUICKLY IN THE OPPOSITE DIRECTION!

**FLITKNOT SPEEDER**
A Geonosian-designed speeder bike used by Count Dooku for high-speed travel across the planet.

52

**WING TURRETS**
Ball turrets enable a wide range of rotation, allowing gunners to strike targets above and below them.

*MMM, CAKE...*

*GET HIM, ANAKIN!*

*WHAT DO YOU THINK I'M DOING— BAKING A CAKE?*

**FLITKNOT SPEEDER**

The Flitknot speeder has appeared in five LEGO sets, ridden by various minifigures.

The speeder is one of very few vehicles on the planet that can be used by non-Geonosians.

" I've never encountered anyone quite as cowardly as the Sith Lord Count Dooku. Well, no, I don't like to hang around when battles break out either. But still... "

# ONE SITH, TWO JEDI

Even though Obi-Wan wants them to fight Dooku together, Anakin rushes to attack first. Dooku blasts Anakin with Force lightning, and then quickly defeats Obi-Wan using the power of the dark side. When Anakin tries to protect his teacher and friend, Dooku swiftly and easily disarms the young Jedi.

**SOLAR SAILER**
The Count's private *Punworcca 116*-class interstellar sloop. Retractable solar sail collects an unknown galactic energy to propel it through space.

*THESE ODDS SEEM A LITTLE UNFAIR.*

**FORCE LIGHTNING**
Electrical Force energy unleashed through the hands. Most commonly employed by agents of the dark side.

BZZZT!

## EPIC DUEL

 In the 2013 set Duel on Geonosis (75017), Count Dooku's Force lightning is stored in a hidden box.

 True to the film, Anakin uses a green LEGO lightsaber because his blue one has been destroyed.

FA-4
Wheeled pilot droid that acts as Count Dooku's chauffeur.

OUCH! FOR US, MAYBE!

# GREEN AND MIGHTY

Once again, Yoda arrives at the last moment to save the day. The diminutive Jedi Master quickly proves that size and age matter little in a duel between two well-trained Force wielders. Knowing that he cannot overcome his whirling, leaping foe, Count Dooku escapes, only by making Yoda stop fighting to save the injured Obi-Wan and Anakin.

GEONOSIS HANGAR
Dooku's secret hangar on Geonosis. The perfect place for a coward to hide his means of escape.

NEVER MY BEST PUPIL WERE YOU, COUNT DOOKU.

TUTAMINIS
The Force-powered ability to absorb and re-channel dangerous forms of energy.

## DUEL ON GEONOSIS

In Duel on Geonosis (set 75017), a control stick can send Yoda leaping through the air as he duels Dooku.

Poggle the Lesser's minifigure is included in this set, although by this point in the movie he is long gone!

OH YEAH? WELL, CHECK OUT WHAT I LEARNED IN SITH LIGHTNING CLASS!

BZZZZT!

COUNT DOOKU
Always elegantly attired, no matter what the circumstances.

# A SECRET WEDDING

The Clone Wars have begun, but romance is blooming, too. During their adventures, Padmé and Anakin have realised that they truly love one another. Although Jedi Knights are forbidden to marry, they are wed in a secret ceremony on Naboo that is witnessed only by their faithful droids, R2-D2 and C-3PO.

## HIDDEN ROMANCE

 A Padmé wedding minifigure is yet to appear, so she will have to make do with her peasant disguise for now!

 Padmé is included in six LEGO sets. In only two of these is she without Anakin.

WE CAN'T TELL ANYONE.

*SNIFF*... WEDDINGS ALWAYS MAKE MY PHOTORECEPTORS LEAK, ARTOO.

C-3PO
An often-worried protocol droid assembled by Anakin Skywalker as a boy.

DING DONG DING DONG

❝Master Anakin gave me to Mistress Padmé as a wedding gift, and she gave Artoo to him. I became the senator's personal assistant and protocol droid, which you must admit is far more befitting my programming than working on a moisture farm!❞

OOPS. MAYBE WE SHOULDN'T HAVE INVITED THREEPIO, THEN...

BEEP WEEOOP.

**FORBIDDEN LOVE**
Both Padmé and Anakin know better than to fall in love, but they can't help it. Still, nothing bad will come of it. Right?

# EPISODE III

## REVENGE OF THE SITH

*War! What is it good for? Count Dooku and a cool new cyborg villain, General Grievous, lead the Separatist Droid Army against the Republic Clone Army.*

*But Chancellor Palpatine has been kidnapped. Oops. Talk about a security breach.*

*Two Jedi Knights are sent to his rescue, although one of them has a worrying habit of disregarding the Jedi rules.....*

# CHANCELLOR KIDNAPPED

The Clone Wars quickly consume the galaxy. On world after world, the Republic's clone troopers battle the Separatists' battle droid army, led by the cybernetic General Grievous. When Grievous captures Chancellor Palpatine in a raid on Coruscant, Anakin and Obi-Wan daringly fly to the rescue.

**BUZZ DROID**
Pistoeka sabotage droid, launched in clusters by Separatist starfighters. The buzz droids attach to enemy vessels and quickly disable their weapons and engines.

**SEPARATIST VULTURE DROID**
Like the Trade Federation version, but bluer.

**DROID TRI-FIGHTER**
A triple-finned Separatist space-superiority starfighter with a gyroscopic core.

## JEDI STARFIGHTER

All but one of the LEGO Eta-2 Jedi starfighters include only the heads of their astromech droid navigators. Only Anakin's green starfighter (set 9494) comes with a complete R2 minifigure.

ANAKIN'S JEDI STARFIGHTER
Eta-2 *Actis*-class light interceptor. A successor to the Delta-7, with greater firepower and opening wing S-foils.

JUST ANOTHER DAY IN THE LIFE OF THE GALAXY'S GREATEST JEDI HERO!

GREAT. GLAD YOU'RE HAVING FUN. NOW... HELP!!

# A DEADLY DECISION

Discovering that the captive Palpatine is being guarded by Count Dooku himself, Anakin resolves that this duel will not end the way their last one did. With Obi-Wan unconscious, Anakin handily defeats Dooku – and at Palpatine's urging, despite his Jedi oath, he finishes off the defeated Sith Lord.

## COUNT DOOKU

 The cape clasp and belt printed on the torso of Count Dooku's minifigure are unique to him.

 The hilt of Dooku's lightsaber is special because it includes a slight curve, just as it does in the movie.

READY TO DUEL, COUNT DOOKU?

**CAPTIVE CHANCELLOR**
Poor Palpatine is Count Dooku's helpless prisoner. So why does he suddenly seem so confident?

YEAH! JUST WATCH THE CAPE. IT'S VERY HARD TO FIND A REPLACEMENT ONLINE.

COUNT DOOKU'S LIGHTSABER
A red-bladed Sith lightsaber with a curved handle for better control. Good for duelling... unless you're up against a very angry Anakin Skywalker.

THE INVISIBLE HAND
Providence-class Separatist destroyer and flagship of General Grievous. Shortly going to crash-land on Coruscant.

# LURE OF THE DARK SIDE

Palpatine's influence over Anakin continues to grow. He makes Anakin start to distrust the Jedi Order and resent its rules. When Anakin worries that a terrible misfortune will befall Padmé, Palpatine tells him that only the Sith have the power to keep loved ones from dying.

**SPACE OPERA**
During a performance of the Mon Calamari ballet Squid Lake at the Galaxies Opera House on Coruscant, Chancellor Palpatine tells Anakin the legend of Darth Plagueis the Wise.

DID I MENTION THAT THE JEDI LIKE KICKING PUPPIES, TOO?

## THE DARK SIDE

There is no Darth Plagueis minifigure, but other ancient Sith exist, including Darth Malgus and Darth Revan.

Anakin's minifigure robes become gradually darker as he travels down the path to the dark side.

SHHHH

I KNEW IT!

66 My poo
completely t
Supreme Ch
words. I, of c
of it. If only
I could have
away from

# CRISIS ON KASHYYYK

The Wookiees of Kashyyyk are under siege by Separatist forces. They have asked the Republic to send help. As a friend to the Wookiees, Yoda leads a clone trooper battalion to defend the planet. Together, Wookiees, clones and Jedi repel the army of droid invaders.

**DWARF SPIDER DROID**
Separatist DSD1 droid that carries a large blaster cannon on four all-terrain legs.

**CORPORATE ALLIANCE TANK DROID**
NR-N99 *Persuader*-class droid enforcer, nicknamed "snail tank". A Separatist droid tank with photoreceptor eyes on stalks.

## KASHYYYK

There are six LEGO sets that include minifigures, droids and vehicles from the Battle of Kashyyyk.

Instructions for a mini Corporate Alliance Tank Droid exist, but the LEGO model has not been released.

# GRIEVOUS FOUND!

Anakin wants to be the one to capture the Separatist commander General Grievous, but the Jedi Council instead sends Obi-Wan to his hideout on the planet Utapau. After a lightsaber fight and a chase across the sinkhole-riddled terrain of Utapau, Obi-Wan destroys Grievous with the cyborg's own blaster.

**WHEEL BIKE**
General Grievous's Tsmeu-6 personal transport vehicle. Walks on four legs, or folds them to roll at high velocity on its central wheel.

I HAVE FOUR ARMS AND A WHEEL WITH LEGS, KENOBI. WHAT HAVE YOU GOT?

**GENERAL GRIEVOUS**
Cunning and merciless cyborg general of the Separatist droid army. Keeps a collection of lightsabers from defeated Jedi. Can split his arms to wield four blades at once.

## GENERAL GRIEVOUS

 General Grievous's minifigure has been released in both tan and white.

 Grievous hates being called a droid, but his original minifigure was built from parts including battle droid arm and leg pieces.

66 That General Grievous was quite a terrible fellow. He led droids into battle and even looked like one, but he wasn't a droid at all. I hear he didn't even like us! Aren't there rules against impersonating a mechanoid? 99

A LIZARD AND THE KNOWLEDGE THAT I'M STILL AROUND IN THE NEXT MOVIE.

**BOGA**
A feathered Utapaun varactyl lizard ridden by Obi-Wan Kenobi in pursuit of General Grievous. She can run and climb sheer rock walls with surprising speed.

# CHOOSING SIDES

Chancellor Palpatine reveals to Anakin that he is the Sith Lord Darth Sidious. Anakin tells Mace Windu what he has learned, but when he sees the two fighting, his fear for Padmé's safety overwhelms him. He attacks Mace, giving the Sith the window of opportunity he needs to slay his sworn enemy.

BZZZT!

YOU SHOULD'VE KNOWN I WAS THE BAD GUY!

**FACE OF THE SITH**
Blasted by his own Force lightning deflected by Mace's lightsaber, Palpatine's true evil visage is seen at last.

CHANCELLOR'S OFFICE
Suite used by the Supreme
Chancellor of the Republic.
Palpatine has decorated it
with Sith art and artefacts,
and keeps his lightsaber
hidden inside a statue.

BUT YOU
WERE ALWAYS
SO POLITE!

## MACE'S WINDOW

Mace's minifigure really has no
choice about his fate: LEGO set
Palpatine's Arrest (set 9526)
includes a window catapult,
designed especially to fling poor
Mace straight out of the window!

# JEDI TEMPLE ATTACK

Palpatine's long and wicked plan is finally falling into place. Now is the time for the end of the Jedi Order. First, he commands his apprentice, once named Anakin Skywalker but now re-named Darth Vader, to lead a legion of clone troopers into the Jedi Temple – and wipe out every last Jedi.

**CLONE TROOPER PHASE II ARMOUR**
Lighter and more comfortable clone armour, with a re-designed helmet and colour-coded unit designations.

ARE YOU SURE THIS IS THE RIGHT ADDRESS, SIR?

**501ST LEGION**
An elite unit of clone troopers, identified by their blue armour markings. Soon to be known as "Vader's Fist".

## 501ST LEGION

Captain Rex often leads the infamous 501st Legion. His clone designation (CT-7567) can be rearranged to form the set number 7675 – the first LEGO set his minifigure appeared in.

WHAT?! I WAS FOLLOWING *YOU!*

**DARTH VADER**
Darth Sidious's new apprentice has sworn his loyalty to the Sith and the dark side of the Force.

# ORDER 66

Next, the Sith Lord sends out a message to all of his clone commanders: they are to immediately execute Order 66, turning against their Jedi Generals. Obi-Wan is caught off guard by a surprise attack from his trusted troops. He barely manages to escape in one piece.

IS THIS BECAUSE I DIDN'T TAKE YOU GUYS WITH ME TO THE BEACH LAST WEEK?

**212TH ATTACK BATTALION**
A unit of clone troopers with orange armour markings. Led by High Jedi General Obi-Wan Kenobi – at least until a moment ago.

## BATTLE OF UTAPAU

 Obi-Wan is usually equipped with a lightsaber, but here he holds the blaster of his just-vanquished foe, General Grievous.

 Commander Cody's minifigure only appears in Phase I clone armour.

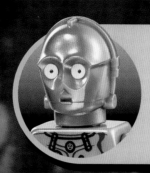

"Talk about long-term planning! Not even I could have suspected that the Republic's own army was programmed to switch allegiances so easily. If I wasn't so horrified, I would have been impressed with the idea."

**COMMANDER CODY**
Leader of the 7th Sky Corps and commander of the 212th Attack Battalion.

I THOUGHT WE WERE GOING HOME EARLY.

NO, THAT'S ORDER 65!

**CLONE PARATROOPER**
Member of the 2nd Airborne Company, with special armour and helmet for high-altitude drops into combat zones.

# BETRAYAL FROM WITHIN

Most of the other Jedi are less fortunate than Obi-Wan. All across the galaxy, clone troopers follow Palpatine's treacherous order. On the tropical, fungus-covered planet Felucia, Jedi Master Aayla Secura is blasted from behind by her own 327th Star Corps.

**FELUCIA**
Outer Rim jungle world. Covered in lots and lots of big, bizarre plants.

**327th STAR CORPS**
Clone trooper corps with yellow-striped armour, sent to fight in the Outer Rim Territories of the galaxy.

READY... AIM...

# THE JEDI PURGE

As he flies his Jedi starfighter through the bridge cities of Cato Neimoidia, Plo Koon has no idea that the clone pilots in his squadron have just received a holographic transmission from the Chancellor. For all the Jedi Master's famed piloting abilities, he cannot evade the lasers that destroy his ship.

**PLO KOON'S JEDI STARFIGHTER**
An older-style Delta-7 starfighter with a custom sky-patterned blue and white paint scheme.

**ARC-170 STARFIGHTER**
Heavy-duty Republic starfighter and bomber flown by clone pilots. S-foils deploy from the top and bottom of each wing.

## PLO KOON

This alien Jedi is one of three minifigures to have a head made from a rubbery material instead of ABS plastic. The other two are also Jedi Masters: Kit Fisto and the Clone Wars version of Yoda.

CATO NEIMOIDIA
A planet with many large, bridged cities. Used as a stronghold by the Trade Federation and other Separatist organisations.

"Oh, what a troubling time for the noble Jedi – so many heroes were lost. In order to forget Palpatine's betrayal, sometimes I wish I could have my memory erased. But no, that's impossible..."

WHAT ARE YOU GUYS SHOOTING AT? IS THERE AN ENEMY SHIP JUST AHEAD OF ME?

PLO KOON
Kel Dor member of the Jedi High Council. Wears a breathing mask and goggles in oxygen-rich atmospheres.

# JEDI REFLEXES

Far away on Kashyyyk, Yoda feels pain as he senses that something terrible has occurred to his Jedi brethren. His great strength in the Force gives him the split-second warning that he needs to defend himself against his double-crossing clones.

HEY, HOW DID YODA KNOW WHAT WE WERE UP TO?

I THINK THE MORE IMPORTANT QUESTION IS: HOW DO WE GET OUT OF HERE?!

**DC-15A BLASTER RIFLE**
Standard clone trooper weapon. Fires 500 shots from a single gas cartridge.

**COMMANDER GREE**
Commander of the 41st Elite Corps, on assignment to the Wookiee homeworld.

**CLONE SCOUT TROOPER**
A member of the camouflage-armoured 41st Elite Corps of clone troopers.

"Master Yoda's escape from Kashyyyk was one of the best kept secrets in the galaxy. Who would have thought that those noisy Wookiees could be so loyal – or so capable of keeping quiet?"

AN UNFORTUNATE TURN OF EVENTS, THIS IS.

# FLIGHT TO MUSTAFAR

Bidding farewell to Padmé, who is as yet unaware of his terrible deeds, Darth Vader obeys his new Master's instructions and flies to the volcanic world of Mustafar to destroy the gathered leaders of the Separatist Alliance. With a single blow, the Clone Wars are ended... but what will be the fate of the Republic?

**DARTH VADER'S JEDI STARFIGHTER**
A green Eta-2 interceptor piloted by Darth Vader on his journey from Coruscant to Mustafar.

THIS PLACE LOOKS NICE...

HEY, I MAY LOOK CRAZY BUT I ALWAYS HAD GOOD TASTE!

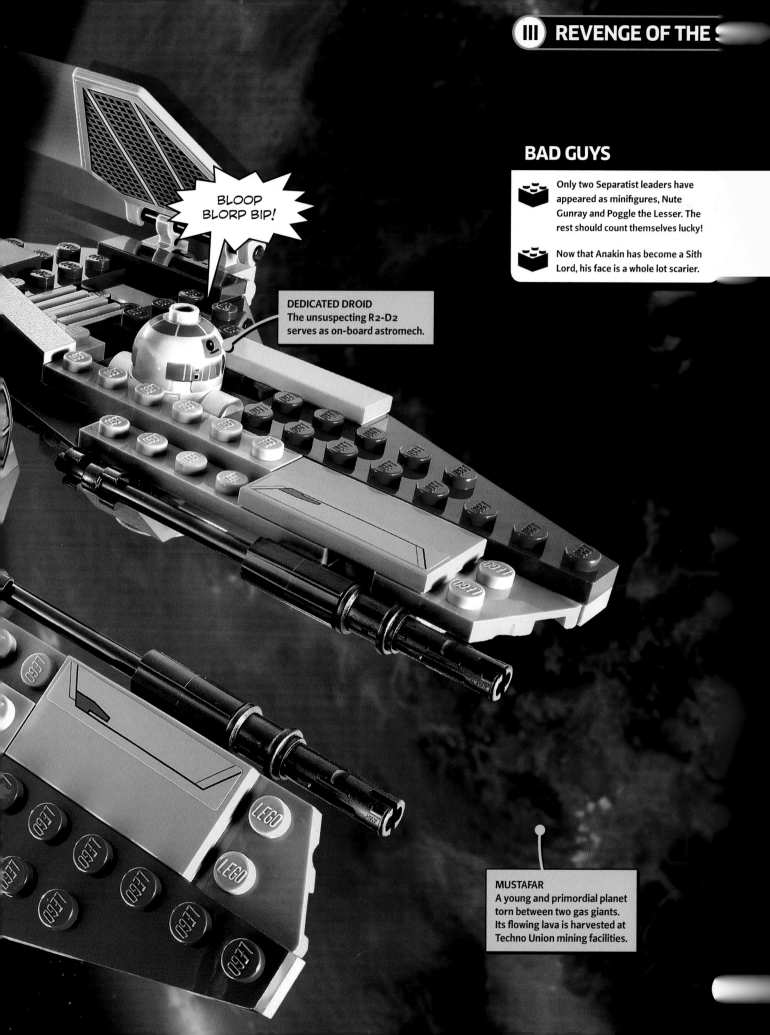

BLOOP BLORP BIP!

DEDICATED DROID
The unsuspecting R2-D2 serves as on-board astromech.

## BAD GUYS

Only two Separatist leaders have appeared as minifigures, Nute Gunray and Poggle the Lesser. The rest should count themselves lucky!

Now that Anakin has become a Sith Lord, his face is a whole lot scarier.

MUSTAFAR
A young and primordial planet torn between two gas giants. Its flowing lava is harvested at Techno Union mining facilities.

# THE NEW ORDER

Palpatine addresses the Senate. Showing his scarred face, he declares that the Jedi Knights have attacked him and betrayed the Republic. To thunderous applause, he announces the Republic's transformation into the Galactic Empire – with himself as its Emperor.

**GRAND CONVOCATION CHAMBER**
A great round room in the Senate Building on Coruscant where the Galactic Senate meets for governmental discussions and debates. From now on, there will be no more debate.

VOTE PALPATINE – BECAUSE YOU DON'T HAVE A CHOICE!

BOO! ER... I MEAN HOORAY!

BRAVO!

HOORAY!

# THE ENEMY REVEALED

Returning to the Jedi Temple, Obi-Wan and Yoda discover what has occurred there. To Obi-Wan's shock and disbelief, a security recording reveals Palpatine's true identity and Anakin's abandonment of the Jedi cause. They know that they have to defeat both of the Sith before it is too late.

## JEDI TEMPLE

 In the LEGO® *Star Wars*™ video game, you must battle clone troopers disguised as Jedi to enter the Temple.

 There are 76 LEGO sets featuring scenes from the Prequel Trilogy, but none feature the Jedi Temple.

I'LL GET YOU, JEDI!

HOLOPROJECTION
Holographic recording of Darth Vader raging through the Jedi Temple, destroying every last Jedi he can find. Not for the faint-hearted.

HOLOPROJECTOR
A device that records, transmits and projects three-dimensional light images and sound... though you may not always like what you see.

66 Master Anakin – my noble Maker. How could he have turned to this? I simply could not believe it! Artoo insists he saw it coming, but I think he's just attention-seeking. Nobody could have predicted this. 99

I CAN'T WATCH THIS! ANAKIN WOULD NEVER DO SOMETHING SO AWFUL!

NOT VERY OBSERVANT, YOU ARE, HMM?

# THE CHALLENGE

Only the greatest of Jedi can stand against the might of the Sith Master. As Yoda enters the office of the new Emperor, the Jedi Master tosses aside the guards with a simple gesture and challenges Darth Sidious to battle. Trading Force blows and lightsaber strikes, the two powerful foes begin their epic struggle.

**HOLDING OFFICE**
Private office of the Chancellor, situated directly below the Galactic Senate Chamber.

> CALLING YOU OUT I AM, "EMPEROR"! SITH ENOUGH TO FIGHT ME, ARE YOU?

> OOF!

**ROYAL GUARD**
Masked, crimson-robed guardsmen whose lives are devoted to protecting the Emperor.

**FORCE PIKE**
An electrically charged weapon that vibrates at high frequencies to stun or shock anything it touches.

## ROYAL GUARDS

 The LEGO force pikes wielded by the royal guards first appeared as spears in 1984!

 The 2014 royal guard minifigures have new fancy capes, with red on one side and dark red on the other.

UM, I HAVE AN URGENT APPOINTMENT... GOTTA RUN!

OW. I DEFINITELY FELT THE FORCE WITH THAT ONE.

# POWER OF THE SITH

Yoda and Sidious's duel takes them into the empty Senate chamber. Although they seem evenly matched, an explosion of Force lightning sends Yoda tumbling to the ground far below. The exhausted Jedi Master has no choice but to go into hiding in the remote outskirts of the galaxy.

**THE SENATE**

There are thousands of *Star Wars* senators, but only seven LEGO senators exist to date: Palpatine, Nute Gunray, Padmé Amidala, Onaconda Farr, Jar Jar Binks, Princess Leia and Mon Mothma.

> GETTING TIRED I AM OF BEING ZAPPED BY FORCE LIGHTNING.

**SENATE POD**
One of over a thousand floating repulsorpods in the Grand Convocation Chamber. Designed more for long, boring speeches than epic Force battles.

# LAVA DUEL

Concerned about Anakin, Padmé follows him to Mustafar – but Obi-Wan sneaks aboard her ship. He hopes to reason with his former friend, but when Darth Vader sees him, his anger makes him lash out at Padmé with the power of the dark side. Seeing that Anakin is completely lost, Obi-Wan battles him on a river of raging lava.

**SITH EYES**
Red and yellow eyes manifested by use of the dark side of the Force.

YOU ALWAYS THOUGHT YOU WERE BETTER THAN ME, OBI-WAN!

**DLC-13 MINING DROID**
A heat-resistant panning droid that – when not being Force-controlled by a furious Sith Lord – scans for and collects minerals from the lava's surface.

DON'T MIND ME, JUST KEEP STANDING ON MY HEAD...

## FIERCE DUEL

 In the 2005 set Ultimate Lightsaber Duel (7257), Anakin and Obi-Wan can be controlled by sticks as they duel.

 7257 is the only LEGO set to include light-up lightsaber versions of Obi-Wan and Anakin's minifigures.

WELL, I'M CERTAINLY BETTER-LOOKING NOW, ANAKIN. HAVE YOU SEEN YOURSELF?

**LAVA SKIFF**
A hovering platform used by Mustafarian lava miners and Jedi duellists to glide safely above the planet's molten lava streams.

# ANAKIN FALLS

Although he cannot rival Vader's strength in the Force, Obi-Wan is very skilled at swordsmanship. Seizing a momentary advantage in the fight, he strikes, leaving Vader badly wounded. Believing the threat of Darth Vader to be over, Obi-Wan picks up Anakin's lightsaber and departs.

## OLD FRIENDS

 Despite being great friends, Anakin and Obi-Wan have appeared in only five LEGO sets together.

 Following this duel, the former Master and Padawan do not meet again until the Death Star set (10188).

OW OW OWWIE OW...

**BEYOND REPAIR**
The force of Obi-Wan's attack leaves Vader's body irreparably damaged. Survival seems unlikely.

**ANAKIN'S LIGHTSABER**
Anakin built this blue-bladed lightsaber himself as a Jedi Knight. He won't be needing it any longer.

## DARTH VADER

- Darth Vader's minifigure has been redesigned 10 times so far!

- Although the rest of his minifigure has changed quite a lot over the years, Darth Vader's iconic helmet remained the same until 2015.

# THE RISE OF DARTH VADER

But Vader's story is far from done. The Emperor finds his injured protégé by the edge of the lava river and brings him back to Coruscant. There, surgical droids repair Vader's body and seal him inside a black mask and armour to keep him alive... although he is now more machine than man.

**FX-6 MEDICAL ASSISTANT DROID**
Multi-armed Medtech Industries "Fixit" droid that assists in Vader's reconstruction.

**DARTH VADER'S ARMOUR**
A sensor-covered, armoured suit and helmet that function as a life-support system. Darth Vader cannot survive without them.

"Well, I can't tell you what's happening here. I can't seem to remember much of anything at all..."

# MASTER AND SERVANT

With the Empire now in charge of the galaxy, Palpatine takes his newest Sith servant to a special project that is under construction, built from the blueprints that Count Dooku brought him years before. Now sworn to the dark side, Darth Vader has no idea that Padmé gave birth to twin children before she died.

> YOU AND ME, KID – WE'RE GOIN' PLACES!

**CONTROL BRIDGE**
With a massive Star Destroyer at his command, Vader can begin his new mission of dominating the galaxy... as the Emperor's right-hand man.

## EMPIRE ERA

As the Republic turns into the Empire, some vehicles are adopted by the new regime. The *Venator*-class cruiser becomes the sinister Star Destroyer, while the ARC-170 starfighter leads to the X-wing of the Rebel Alliance.

**DEATH STAR PLANS**
Hologram displaying top secret plans for the Death Star, the Empire's ultimate weapon of galactic domination. Approximate time to completion: 19 years.

"Neither Vader nor the Emperor knew that Obi-Wan had hidden the newborn Skywalker twins on — wait, didn't I get my memory erased right after returning from Mustafar? How am I even telling you about this? Pardon me, but I think I need to shut down for a while..."

BUT NOT BACK TO TATOOINE, RIGHT? I HATE IT THERE.

# EPISODE IV

## A NEW HOPE

*Now it's the rebels versus the Empire.*

*Civil war... blah blah blah... politics... blah... And the Empire has a DEATH STAR!*

*A plucky (or maybe crazy, brave or TOTALLY INSANE) princess named Leia has stolen the top-secret Death Star plans. Can she pass these on to the Rebel Alliance while avoiding capture? Can she? CAN SHE??*

# IMPERIAL PURSUIT

Although the Galactic Empire rules supreme, some still fight against it. An alliance of rebels, striking from a secret base, has stolen the plans to the Emperor's ultimate weapon. Darth Vader's massive Star Destroyer hunts down the rebel ship carrying the plans as it flees towards a certain desert planet.

## STAR DESTROYER

 An impressive six Star Destroyer models have been released, ranging in length from a few centimetres to almost a metre!

 The 2014 Imperial Star Destroyer (set 75055) has 1,359 pieces.

**STAR DESTROYER**
A huge Imperial warship stretching 1.6 km (1 mile) long. Bristling with turbolaser turrets, ion cannons and tractor beams.

**TATOOINE**
An unremarkable sandy world in the Outer Rim where surprisingly important things keep happening.

EAT OUR SPACE-DUST, IMPERIALS! HA-HA-HA!

DON'T TEASE 'EM, MAN.

*TANTIVE IV*
A Corellian "blockade runner" CR90 corvette. Officially used for diplomatic missions, but covertly helping the Rebel Alliance against the Empire.

# REBEL DEFENDERS

The rebel troopers are loyal and brave, but they cannot stop Imperial stormtroopers from boarding the ship. The troopers capture its prize passenger, Princess Leia of Alderaan... but only after she hides the plans and a special message inside a resourceful astromech droid.

**CAPTAIN ANTILLES**
The steadfast Raymus Antilles, captain of the *Tantive IV*.

HEY, THE PRINCESS JUST TOLD THAT DROID A SECRET! CAN I HEAR THE SECRET TOO?

ER... MAYBE LATER.

**PRINCESS LEIA**

Some of the Princess Leia minifigures released in 2009's *Tantive IV* set (10198) included a hair piece without the usual texturing. This minifigure has become sought after by collectors.

**PRINCESS LEIA**
Leia Organa of the Royal House of Alderaan. Princess, senator and secret member of the Rebel Alliance.

THERE'S A MISTER VADER AT THE DOOR. SHOULD I LET HIM IN?

"I lost track of Artoo for a moment during the battle. When I found him, an important-looking passenger was speaking to him. Then, without bothering to explain what was going on, he had the nerve to launch us both in an escape pod!"

**REBEL TROOPER**
Volunteer soldier in the resistance against the Empire.

# DROID ESCAPE

Launched to safety aboard an escape pod, the droids R2-D2 and C-3PO crash-land in the sandy wasteland of Tatooine. R2 wants to complete his mission for the princess, while poor bewildered C-3PO has no idea what is going on or how he has ended up in this mess.

**DUNE SEA**
Enormous desert. Known for sand dunes, Tusken Raiders, Jawa scavengers and not much else.

YOU KNOW, ARTOO, I'M STARTING TO THINK YOU DON'T EVEN *HAVE* AN ESCAPE POD FLYING LICENSE.

**ESCAPE POD**
A small, utilitarian travel pod designed to let passengers and crew evacuate from damaged starships. Not usually intended (or permitted) for droid use.

BREET-BEDOOP!

HISSSSSSSS

## ESCAPE POD

Two LEGO sets have been released featuring C-3PO, R2-D2 and their escape pod. Although it is a tight squeeze, the droids from the 2012 set should consider themselves lucky. The 2001 escape pod did not have any seats inside!

# A FATEFUL MEETING

While lost in the desert, R2-D2 and C-3PO are caught by Jawas. Their captivity does not last long, however. Owen Lars, a Tatooine moisture farmer, visits the Jawas' sandcrawler to buy some used droids for his farm. He brings his nephew with him – a boy named Luke Skywalker.

**SAND**
It's coarse and rough and irritating, and it gets everywhere. Tatooine has a lot of it.

CAN I GET A DISCOUNT ON THE SHORT ONE?

**JAWA**
Small, hooded technology scavengers with glowing eyes. They "find" and sell old droids and other junked equipment.

UTINNI!

IS THAT A YES OR A NO?

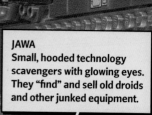

# LEIA'S MESSAGE

R2-D2 leads Luke and C-3PO to Obi-Wan Kenobi, now an old desert hermit. Obi-Wan tells Luke that his father had once been a great Jedi Knight, and gives him Anakin's lightsaber. Having found the one he had been sent to find, R2-D2 plays Leia's message: a plea for help in the fight against the Empire.

WHAT DO YOU WANT, DROIDS I'VE DEFINITELY NEVER MET BEFORE?

"OLD BEN" KENOBI
A hermit who lives in the dune wastes of Tatooine. He is actually the fugitive Jedi Obi-Wan Kenobi. Shhh, don't tell the Empire!

A PRINCESS, EH? SO WHY DOES SHE LOOK SO FAMILIAR?

## "OLD BEN" KENOBI

"Old Ben" appears in five sets, and has had the same hair piece all five times.

Obi-Wan is in hiding, but his minifigure is not disguised very well – he is still wearing his Jedi robes!

HELP ME, OBI-WAN KENOBI, YOU'RE MY ONLY... WAIT, AM I STANDING ON A TABLE?! THIS IS NO WAY TO PROJECT A PRINCESS!

**HOLOGRAPHIC LEIA**
In her holographic recording, Leia asks Obi-Wan to take R2-D2 and the Death Star plans inside him to her adoptive father on Alderaan.

# PRISONER OF THE EMPIRE

Princess Leia is in big trouble. Locked inside a prison cell on the Death Star, she is questioned by Darth Vader. He demands to know the location of the rebel base. But no matter what the Sith Lord does, the fearless princess refuses to talk.

**DEATH STAR TROOPER**
Members of the Imperial Navy who serve aboard the invincible Death Star battle station. A great job if you can get it.

I HEAR IT'S HOTH DOGS FOR SUPPER IN THE CANTEEN TONIGHT.

WELL, ANYTHING'S BETTER THAN DIANOGA OMELETTE AGAIN.

**STORMTROOPER**
The Empire's highly-trained, armoured soldiers. The successors to clone troopers. Supposedly excellent shots.

114

# DESTINATION: MOS EISLEY

Luke finds out that stormtroopers have followed the droids back to his farm. With no home left to return to, he agrees to travel to Alderaan with Obi-Wan and learn to be a Jedi like his father. Together with R2-D2 and C-3PO, they take Luke's landspeeder to the spaceport town of Mos Eisley.

## LANDSPEEDER

 Landspeeders have been included in four LEGO sets, ranging all the way from 1999 to 2014. Their colours have varied over the years, going from tan, to sand red and finally to flesh, a dark sandy colour.

**SANDTROOPER**
Imperial stormtroopers with special armour and equipment for operating in desert environments.

> WE'RE LOOKING FOR SOME DROIDS.

**LUKE'S LANDSPEEDER**
An old-model X-34 repulsorlift speeder. Missing one engine cover. Has seen better days.

**66** I am still not entirely sure how we got past those sandtroopers. Master Kenobi just raised his hand and they let us go along on our way. It was most peculiar! **99**

SENTRY SPY DROID
Imperial droids that float around with a camera and transmitter, looking for anything suspicious.

BE-DEEP

DROIDS? WHAT DROIDS? WE HAVEN'T SEEN ANY DROIDS. NOPE, NO DROIDS HERE!

JEDI MIND TRICK
An ancient method for clouding the thoughts of the weak-willed with the Force.

FOR SOME REASON, I BELIEVE HIM!

BLEEEEEP!

# THE CANTINA

The Mos Eisley Cantina is full of music and aliens from many worlds. It is a perilous place for a young farm boy like Luke, but he needs to find a starship captain who is willing to take him and his friends to Alderaan.

**GREEDO**
Rodian bounty hunter who is about to threaten Han Solo. This bad idea will be his last.

ANY SONG REQUESTS, GUYS?

DO YOU KNOW THERE'S A DEWBACK OVER THERE?

NOPE, BUT IF YOU HUM IT, WE'LL PLAY IT.

**FIGRIN D'AN AND THE MODAL NODES**
An all-Bith band that has recently fallen on hard times.

"As soon as Artoo and I stepped inside the cantina, a light started flashing and the bartender said that we had to leave. Why would anyone want to keep out droids? We're always so helpful and polite. Well, except Artoo sometimes."

**CANTINA**

Two LEGO models of the Cantina have been released, but neither includes the bartender, Wuher.

The Bith musicians are just one of 48 alien species released in the LEGO® *Star Wars*™ range so far!

**MOS EISLEY CANTINA**
A popular hangout for any smugglers, bounty hunters and general lowlifes unfortunate enough to end up on Tatooine.

THE OTHER GUYS GET SPEEDER BIKES AND WHAT DO I GET...

ANYONE SEEN A GUY CALLED HAN SOLO?

DEWBACK DO THIS, DEWBACK DO THAT!

**DEWBACK**
An omnivorous Tatooine lizard, domesticated for use as a sandtrooper mount.

119

# HAN SOLO

Han Solo is a smuggler who is in debt to his former employer, Jabba the Hutt. Together with his Wookiee copilot, Chewbacca, he agrees to transport Luke, Obi-Wan and the droids. The only problem is that when they reach Alderaan, it isn't there. The Death Star has blown it up. Oh dear.

*MILLENNIUM FALCON*
A frequently-rebuilt YT-1300 light freighter. Equipped with lots of secret compartments, quad-laser turrets and a less-than-reliable hyperdrive.

WROOOAGH!*
*TRANSLATION: HI.

CHEWBACCA
Han's best pal and trusty copilot. A 200-year-old Wookiee with a big heart and a short temper.

## MILLENNIUM FALCON

 The Ultimate Collector's Series *Millennium Falcon* (set 10179) is the largest LEGO *Star Wars* set ever!

 Just like in the movies, minifigures must bend down when boarding the *Falcon* to avoid bumping their heads.

DOCKING BAY 94
One of Mos Eisley's numerous docking bays. Right next to docking bay 93. Rented by Han Solo for 25 credits per day.

66 I remember when I first met Captain Solo and his Wookiee copilot. I thought they were rather impolite to Master Luke, but it wasn't my place to say. Some would call their piloting skills impressive, but not me. I would call them terrifying. 99

THIS HERE'S THE FALCON. SHE MAY NOT LOOK LIKE MUCH, BUT SHE'S MADE FROM 5,197 PIECES AND TOOK ME 16 STRAIGHT HOURS TO BUILD.

HAN SOLO
A Corellian starship captain with a ramshackle ship, a price on his head and a willingness to not ask his passengers any questions... for the right price.

121

# THE TRASH COMPACTOR

The *Millennium Falcon* is caught and pulled into the Death Star. Disguised as stormtroopers, Luke and Han find Princess Leia and break her out of her cell – but they land in even bigger danger when they wind up inside a trash compactor. They only avoid being flattened with R2-D2 and C-3PO's help.

## TRASH COMPACTOR

 This iconic scene appears in just one LEGO set, Death Star (10188).

 A LEGO minifigure, made of the standard ABS plastic, could withstand 431 kg (950 lbs) of pressure before being crushed.

STORMTROOPER DISGUISE
Very useful for infiltrating an Imperial stronghold. Not so useful for escaping from a trash compactor.

AAAARGH!*
*TRANSLATION: AAAARGH!

PUSHING?! WHOOPS – I'VE BEEN PULLING!

DIANOGA
A hungry one-eyed, tentacled creature that lurks in the water at the bottom of the trash compactor.

# OBI-WAN'S SACRIFICE

Obi-Wan Kenobi faces Darth Vader one last time. He allows Vader to defeat him but disappears as the final lightsaber blow is struck, becoming one with the Force. His sacrifice lets the others escape. They fly to the rebel base with the plans, and just in time – because the Death Star is on its way.

**DEATH STAR HANGAR**
Obi-Wan has to do something to help Luke and the others reach the guarded *Millennium Falcon*. His duel with Darth Vader is just the thing to get the stormtroopers' attention.

WHSHHHH... VZZZMMMM... KRSSHH!

"What bravery Obi-Wan Kenobi displayed! Master Luke was very upset that his mentor was gone. I was pretty upset, too. Without Master Kenobi, there was nobody to keep law and order on board the *Millennium Falcon*."

**DARTH VADER'S LIGHTSABER**
Built by Darth Vader 19 years ago, following his previous

# X-WING ASSAULT

Luke has never piloted a starfighter before, but the rebels need all the help they can get. He joins a squadron of X-wings as they launch a desperate attack on the Death Star's only vulnerable point. The battle station's defences are strong, and soon Luke's ship is the only one left.

**MERIDIAN TRENCH**
Deep trench on the surface of the Death Star. Location of the Death Star's weakest point – a thermal exhaust port near the north pole of the battle station.

USE THE FORCE, LUKE!

OBI-WAN? IS THAT YOU?

EITHER THAT OR YOUR SHIP IS LEAKING OXYGEN FAST.

**SPIRIT OF OBI-WAN KENOBI**
Obi-Wan's body may be gone, but his spirit and wisdom live on through the Force.

## X-WING FIGHTER

 The X-Wing Fighter (set 7140, 1999) was the first set ever to be released in the LEGO *Star Wars* line.

 There are seven X-wing pilot minifigures, including Luke, Jek Porkins and Biggs Darklighter.

**TIE FIGHTER**
Named for their twin ion engines, TIE starfighters make up most of the Empire's space combat forces. An individual TIE is easily destroyed, but a group can be very dangerous.

**X-WING FIGHTER**
The Incom T-65 X-wing starfighter is the Rebel Alliance's best and most versatile snub fighter. Its laser-cannon-tipped S-foil wings open into a distinctive X-shape.

# DEATH STAR DESTROYED

Luke is nearly shot down by Darth Vader in his TIE Advanced fighter, but a last-second save by Han Solo in the *Millennium Falcon* gives him the chance he needs. With his aim guided by the Force, Luke fires two proton torpedoes right into the Death Star's exhaust port. The Empire's ultimate weapon blows up in a spectacular explosion.

HOORAY! WE'LL NEVER HAVE TO WORRY ABOUT A DEATH STAR EVER AGAIN!

THE DEATH STAR
Innumerable turbolasers. 7,000 defensive starfighters. A planet-destroying superlaser. As big as a small moon. One tiny weak spot.

KA-THOOOM!

**FIRST DEATH STAR**

 The LEGO Death Star might have actually survived Luke's attack, had it not been for the addition of proton torpedoes to the 2012 X-Wing Starfighter set (9493)!

# THE HEROES' REWARD

In reward for their heroism, Luke and Han are presented with medals by Princess Leia at a rebel award ceremony. R2-D2, damaged during the battle, is fixed up, too. But even though they have won their first true victory over the Empire, they know that there are still many challenges yet to come.

> PSSST... SHOULDN'T CHEWIE GET A MEDAL, TOO?

> I ASKED, BUT HE SAID HE'D RATHER HAVE A STEAK.

**MEDAL OF BRAVERY**
The highest award that can be bestowed upon a hero of the rebellion.

**TEMPLE STEPS**

The Massassi constructed hundreds of steps when building their ancient temples.

**ROYAL AWARD CEREMONY**
Conducted by Princess Leia inside the ancient Massassi Temple on the moon of Yavin 4, the previously-secret home base of the Rebel Alliance.

"This was one of the most enjoyable ceremonies that I have ever attended. Artoo and I were so polished and clean! I suppose the others looked nice as well. For humans, that is."

OOOAGH!*
*TRANSLATION: YAY!

**BANDOLIER**
Bandolier filled with ammo is never removed – even during a medal ceremony!

# EPISODE V

## THE EMPIRE STRIKES BACK

*It is a dark time for the rebellion. Maybe it's night. Hard to tell in space.*

*A group of rebels, led by Luke Skywalker, has set up a secret base on the planet Hoth.*

*There's nothing else there but ice, however, so they might be quite easy to find....*

# ECHO BASE

Since the destruction of the Death Star, the Empire
has pursued the Rebel Alliance across the galaxy.
The rebels take refuge on the inhospitable ice planet
Hoth, surrounded by an asteroid belt. Here, they dig
out a new secret base that they hope will be safe
from the prying eyes of Imperial spies.

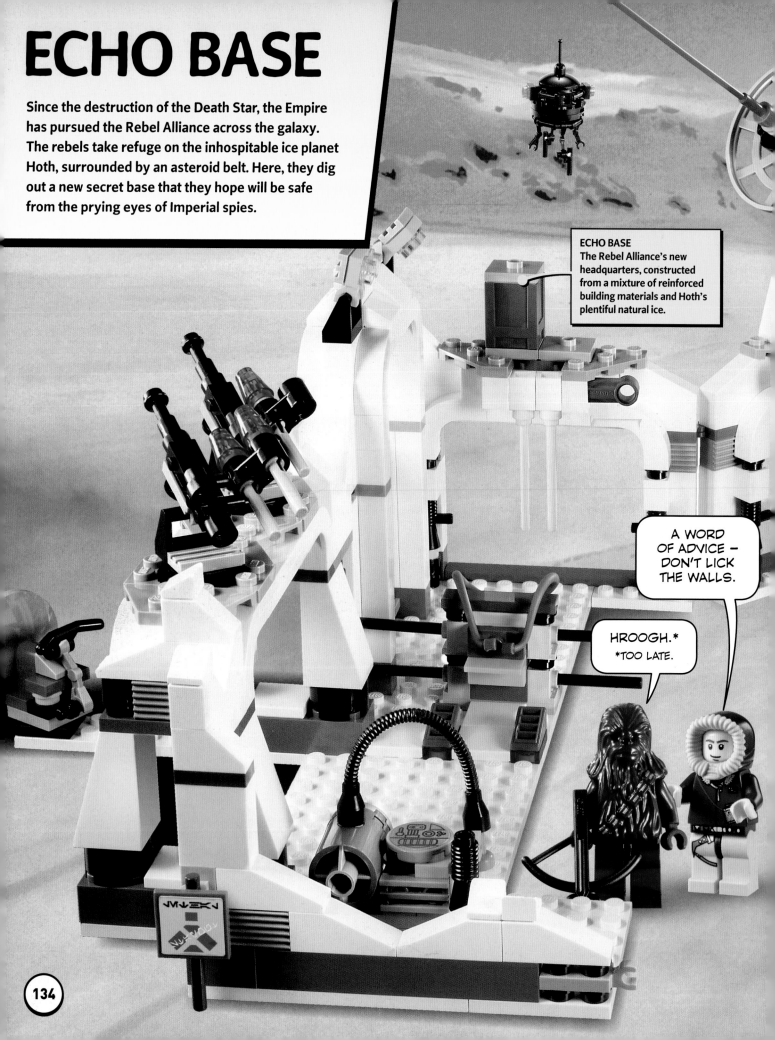

**ECHO BASE**
The Rebel Alliance's new
headquarters, constructed
from a mixture of reinforced
building materials and Hoth's
plentiful natural ice.

A WORD
OF ADVICE –
DON'T LICK
THE WALLS.

HROOGH.*
*TOO LATE.

"Of all the rebel bases we inhabited, I think that Echo Base was my least favourite. My actuators kept freezing up, and there was that very unfortunate misunderstanding with the heating units in the princess's quarters..."

**2-1B**
Medical droid and Echo Base's resident doctor.

**BACTA TANK**
A tank filled with a gelatinous goo that rapidly heals injuries.

**TAUNTAUN**
Part mammal, part reptile, and one of the only species that can live in Hoth's freezing climate – though everything has its limits.

# ECHO BASE

Princess Leia's minifigure takes advantage of Hoth's icy climate as she eats a LEGO ice lolly.

The Aurebesh text on the LEGO warning signs around Echo Base reads: "Lethal – stay out".

# WAMPA'S LAIR, BEWARE!

While out on patrol, Luke spots something coming down from the sky. Before he can investigate, he is attacked by a shaggy white beast called a wampa. It sticks Luke to the roof of its cave and is about to make a frozen snack out of him when Luke uses the Force to summon his lightsaber.

MMMM, ICED REBEL. MY FAVOURITE!

**WAMPA**
A large predator native to Hoth. Its white fur camouflages it against the snow, while it waits for prey to wander near.

## THE WAMPA

The wampa has the same horn pieces as the tauntaun – marking both out as inhabitants of Hoth.

Although a rather common sight on Hoth, the LEGO wampa has only been spotted in one set (8089).

"When Master Luke failed to return, Captain Solo went out looking for him on a tauntaun. Thank goodness they made it back all right! Well, apart from the tauntaun, who I am told was very helpful in the rescue."

SKELETON
A former prisoner of the wampa – evidently severely lacking in Force powers.

C'MON, LET ME DOWN! I'M A VERY IMPORTANT HERO WITH A BIG DESTINY THAT I'M PRETTY SURE DOESN'T INVOLVE BEING EATEN.

FORMER TAUNTAUN
One of the wampa's earlier meals.

# AT-AT ATTACK

The object that Luke had seen in the sky turned out to be an Imperial probe droid. Now the Empire knows where the rebels are. Their Star Destroyers deploy colossal Imperial AT-AT walkers, which stomp across the snow towards Echo Base. Luke and his fellow pilots try to hold them off with their (much smaller) snowspeeders.

**SNOWSPEEDER**
A T-47 airspeeder adapted for cold-weather flight. Rear-mounted launcher fires a magnetic harpoon and tow cable that can be used to ensnare an Imperial walker's legs.

GUYS, GUYS! I'VE GOT A HILARIOUS IDEA. DID ANY OF YOU EVER TIE YOUR FRIENDS' SHOELACES TOGETHER WHEN YOU WERE KIDS?

## AT-AT WALKERS

 The imposing AT-AT has appeared in five LEGO sets. One version is motorised (set 10178).

 The largest AT-AT model stands tall at 30 cm (12 in), towering over any nearby minifigures.

**AT-AT WALKER**
All Terrain Armoured Transports, gigantic mobile walkers used by the Empire to carry troops and demolish key enemy targets. Slow, but practically unstoppable, as long as they're upright.

# IMPERIAL INVASION

Although the rebels fight well, they are no match for an Imperial onslaught. The walkers destroy their power generator, and snowtroopers break through the walls of Echo Base. Knowing that they cannot win, Princess Leia gives the command for all rebels to evacuate the base.

**E-WEB BLASTER**
Tripod-mounted heavy repeating blaster cannon used by the Empire. Powered by a connected generator box.

**SNOWTROOPER**
Cold-assault Imperial stormtroopers with heated, insulated armour and breather hoods.

VIPER PROBE DROID
Deep-space reconnaisance droid used by the Empire. Equipped with floodlights, multiple arms and a self-destruct function.

FOOOM!

SNOWTROOPERS HAVE ENTERED THE BASE!

GENERAL RIEEKAN
Commander of Echo Base. A fearless general who leads the rebel troops into icy battle.

"NO TROOPERS"? WHAT ARE YOU TALKING ABOUT?! THEY'RE RIGHT HERE!

R-3PO
Moody protocol droid stationed at Echo Base. Programmed to detect infiltration attempts.

141

# SEPARATE PATHS

Han, Leia, Chewie and C-3PO blast off from Hoth on board the *Millennium Falcon*, but Luke and R2-D2 fly their X-wing in a different direction. When he was out in the snow, Luke had received a message from the Force spirit of Obi-Wan Kenobi. Obi-Wan told Luke to travel to the planet Dagobah to learn from a great Jedi Master. So off Luke goes.

THE *EXECUTOR*
Darth Vader's command flagship, a Super Star Destroyer. Twelve times the length of a standard Imperial Star Destroyer. Not a vessel to be trifled with.

OKAY, YOU KEEP THOSE STAR DESTROYERS OCCUPIED WHILE I GO GET MAGIC POWERS.

HOTH
Honestly, nobody's going to miss this place.

> "I was glad to get away from Hoth after nearly freezing my gears off. Do pardon my terribly rude language, but it really was very cold. Still, I worried about Master Luke travelling all that way with only Artoo."

SPACE
Still black, and still full of stars.

THAT SEEMS...
FAIR...

## LEGO® PLANETS

The LEGO Planets series includes miniature models of 10 planets (including two versions of Endor). There is also a miniature Death Star and an asteroid field as part of the same series.

# ASTEROID FIELD

The Empire is hot on the *Millennium Falcon*'s tail. Han tries to jump to lightspeed, but the ship's hyperdrive has been damaged. Taking a dangerous risk, he flies into a nearby asteroid field to hide and make repairs – almost getting the *Falcon* swallowed by a giant space slug in the process.

**ASTEROID FIELD**
A terrifying gauntlet of spinning, hurtling space rocks. No sane starship captain would even think of going inside.

**TIE BOMBER**
Double-hulled TIE fighter armed with an assortment of missiles, torpedoes and other explosive warheads.

## ASTEROID FIELD

The 2013 LEGO asteroid field model (set 75008) comes with a TIE pilot minifigure and a mini TIE bomber.

If the space slug from the movie was built to scale in LEGO bricks, it would be over 20 m (66 feet) long!

"No one ever seems to appreciate it when I tell them their odds of survival. Human beings are a truly mysterious species."

CAPTAIN SOLO, THE ODDS OF SURVIVING THIS ASTEROID FIELD ARE 3,720 TO ONE.

WHAT? WHY DIDN'T YOU TELL ME THAT BEFORE I FLEW IN HERE?!

# OLD JEDI MASTER

Luke tries to land on the planet Dagobah, but his X-wing sinks into a swamp. Even more annoyingly, he meets a strange green creature who will not tell him where to find the Jedi Master he seeks. Luke is astounded when he finally realises that this wrinkly little guy is Yoda, his new Jedi teacher.

**YODA'S HUT**
The Jedi Master's simple dwelling on Dagobah. Built from mud and parts of his old escape pod.

**GNARLTREE**
Unique to Dagobah. These trees thrive in swamplands.

# VADER'S TASK

Aboard his Super Star Destroyer, the *Executor*, Darth Vader kneels before a holographic projection of the Emperor. Palpatine warns Vader of the danger that Luke Skywalker could be if he becomes a Jedi. Vader promises that he will turn Luke to the dark side instead.

HMMM... YOU'RE SURE YOU CAN DO IT?

**EMPEROR HOLOGRAM**
The Emperor chooses to project himself at a larger-than-life size to emphasise the power he has over his servant.

# THE *EXECUTOR*

The Ultimate Collector's Series Super Star Destroyer (set 10221) is the longest of all LEGO® *Star Wars*™ sets. Built from 3,152 pieces, it measures nearly 127 cm (50 in) long!

**HOLOPROJECTION CHAMBER**
A room on the *Executor* near Darth Vader's meditation pod, where Vader receives long-range communications from the Emperor.

TRUST ME, BOSS! WHEN HAVE I EVER LET YOU DOWN? (EXCEPT FOR THAT WHOLE DEATH STAR THING...)

AND WHAT
TODAY HAVE
YOU LEARNED?

# JEDI TRAINING

Luke's Jedi lessons begin. He carries Yoda
through the swamps in order to push beyond
his physical limits. He stands on his head
and practises moving things with the Force
– including unwilling astromech droids.
The young Jedi also learns that the dark
side leads to anger, fear and aggression.

**AIRBORNE ASTROMECH**
Even droids can fly thanks to the
power of the Force – a trick that
just may come in handy later on.

# BOUNTY PARTY

Darth Vader knows that the quickest way to catch Luke is to track down his friends. So he hires a pack of bounty hunters, including the infamous Boba Fett, to find the *Millennium Falcon*. Fett locates the *Falcon* and follows it to the gas-mining colony of Cloud City on Bespin. Now Vader can lay his trap.

**BOBA FETT**
The son of Jango Fett has grown up to be the galaxy's most dreaded and capable bounty hunter. No one escapes from Boba Fett.

SERIOUSLY, NO DISINTEGRATIONS.

WHAT IF I JUST DISINTEGRATE THEM A LITTLE?

NO!

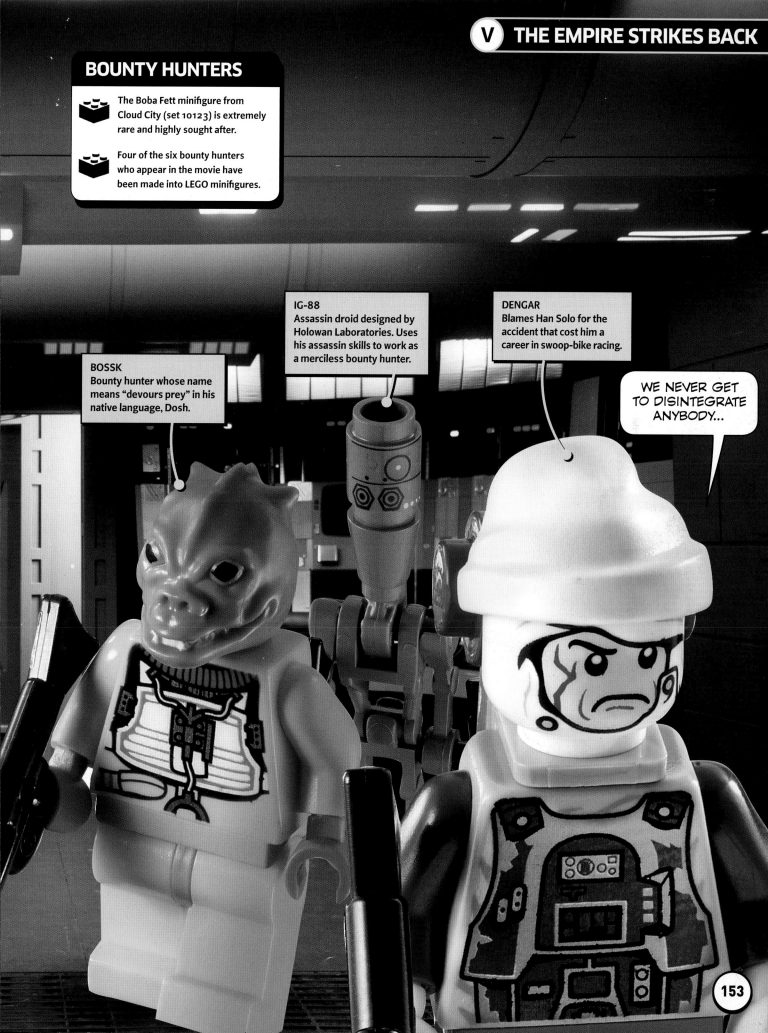

BOUNTY HUNTERS

The Boba Fett minifigure from Cloud City (set 10123) is extremely rare and highly sought after.

Four of the six bounty hunters who appear in the movie have been made into LEGO minifigures.

IG-88
Assassin droid designed by Holowan Laboratories. Uses his assassin skills to work as a merciless bounty hunter.

DENGAR
Blames Han Solo for the accident that cost him a career in swoop-bike racing.

BOSSK
Bounty hunter whose name means "devours prey" in his native language, Dosh.

WE NEVER GET TO DISINTEGRATE ANYBODY...

# HEAVY LIFTING

Luke doesn't think he will ever be able to lift something as heavy as his X-wing out of the swamp. Yoda uses the Force to lift the ship into the air, showing his Jedi trainee how much he has left to learn. Suddenly, Luke senses that his friends are in trouble. He flies off, despite Yoda's warning that leaving before his training is complete will lead to disaster.

**ENGINE**
Incom 4L4 fusial thrust engine has not yet rusted over from the swamp water.

SO IF SIZE DOESN'T MATTER, HOW COME YOU HAD SO MUCH TROUBLE WITH THAT BIG PILLAR IN EPISODE II?

**SWAMP**
Once something falls into this muck, it rarely comes out again. An exception is droids, which the submerged carnivores find unappetising.

## SWAMPED

 The 2004 and 2006 models of the X-wing are nearly identical. The 2004 version comes with foliage.

 X-Wing Fighter (set 4502) is the only LEGO set to feature Yoda as portrayed in the Original Trilogy.

66 Artoo was rather concerned for his safety on this remote planet. However, Master Luke was right in assuring him that the planet is perfectly safe for droids. Luckily, swamp creatures dislike the taste of metal! 99

### THE FORCE
A mystical, invisible energy created by and binding together all living things. Those who can sense and control it can perform seemingly impossible feats.

ASK TOO MANY QUESTIONS, YOU DO.

### SWAMP PLANTS
Dagobah is teeming with lush plant life. The bogs are filled with greenery that covers anything that lands in the water.

# DEEP FREEZE

On floating Cloud City, Han Solo meets up with his old friend Lando Calrissian. But the Empire has arrived there first, so the rebels are betrayed and captured. Han Solo is frozen inside a block of carbonite and given to Boba Fett to bring to Jabba the Hutt. Vader plans to capture and freeze Luke the same way.

## LANDO CALRISSIAN
Former gambler, current Baron Administrator of Cloud City and previous owner of the *Millennium Falcon*. Not completely trustworthy, but not completely untrustworthy either.

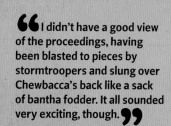

" I didn't have a good view of the proceedings, having been blasted to pieces by stormtroopers and slung over Chewbacca's back like a sack of bantha fodder. It all sounded very exciting, though. "

## CARBONITE

 The original Han Solo in carbonite was a printed 2 x 1 x 5 LEGO brick. The new version is a unique mould.

 Han Solo's minifigure can be placed inside the new carbonite piece as though he has been frozen inside.

CARBONITE
Carbon plus tibanna gas plus pressure plus extreme cold equals a block of metal alloy that can flash-freeze food, supplies – and rebel prisoners at an acceptable level of risk.

# THE DUEL

When Luke arrives on Cloud City, Darth Vader is waiting for him. Igniting their lightsabers, they begin to duel. Vader tries to trap Luke, but Luke's newly learned Jedi skills save him. Vader uses his own Force powers to hurl heavy objects at Luke and knock him through a window.

TIME TO GET EVEN WITH THE GUY WHO KILLED MY DAD!

**CARBON-FREEZING CHAMBER**
A facility on Cloud City where objects are frozen in carbonite for easy transportation. Usually operated by trained Ugnaught workers, but a Sith Lord's Force powers work just as well.

## CLOUD CITY

 Cloud City's Ugnaught inhabitants appear in the LEGO *Star Wars* video game, but not as actual minifigures.

 2003's Cloud City (set 10123) is one of the rarest and most sought after LEGO *Star Wars* sets.

**LIGHTSABER**
The primary weapon of a Jedi or Sith, created by a plasma blade focused through a crystal within the hilt. Blue or green, usually, for good guys, red for bad guys.

KZZZCH!

BOY, ARE YOU IN FOR A SURPRISE...

# "I AM YOUR FATHER"

Luke quickly realises that he is no match for the Sith Lord. Vader's lightsaber skills are exceptional, and Luke begins to falter. As the battered and bruised rebel hero retreats along a high maintenance catwalk, Vader has one more shock in store. He reveals that he, Darth Vader, is Luke's father.

## FATHER AND SON

 It can hardly be a surprise that Anakin and Luke are related, they often wear the same hair piece!

 Despite being two of the most common minifigures, Vader and Luke appear together in only four sets.

**A FATHER'S HOPE**
Darth Vader believes that with Luke on his side, they can remove the Emperor from power – leaving father and son to rule the galaxy together.

YOU SEE, FIRST THERE WAS THIS PODRACE ON TATOOINE...

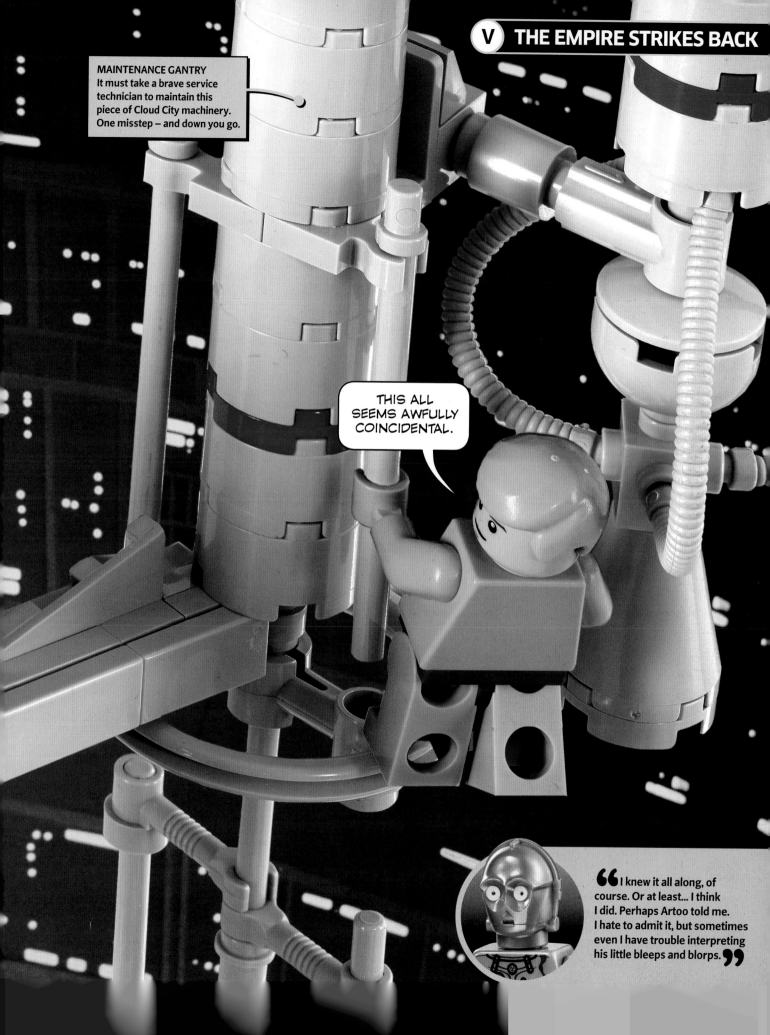

# LUKE'S CHOICE

At first, Luke cannot believe it. How can Darth Vader be Anakin Skywalker, the Jedi hero? But the Force tells him that it is the truth. Raising a fist, Vader invites Luke to join him on the dark side. He tells Luke he has no other choice, but Vader is wrong. Luke lets go and plunges to his apparent doom.

## AIR SHAFT

 The Cloud City air shaft is not depicted in any LEGO set – it would require too many bricks!

 Though Luke was lucky to survive a fall from such a height, LEGO bricks are incredibly hard to break.

> OKAY, I GENUINELY WAS NOT EXPECTING YOU TO DO THAT.

AIR SHAFT
Jedi can live through some tough situations, but a 60,000 km (37,000 mile) fall probably isn't one of them.

I'M NOT SURE IT WAS SUCH A GOOD IDEA MYSEEEEELF!

LUKE SKYWALKER
The shock of Darth Vader's revelation isn't enough to make Luke sway from his allegiance to the Jedi.

# A CALL HEEDED

Clinging to a weather vane beneath Cloud City, Luke calls out with the Force. Princess Leia hears Luke's voice as she flies in the *Millennium Falcon*. With Lando's aid, she and the others have escaped from the Empire's guards. Leia guides the ship to help Luke on board.

> HERE WE COME, LUKE!

**CLOUDS OF BESPIN**
Far below, the huge, uninhabitable planet Bespin is mined for its valuable gases.

## RESCUE

Getting on board the *Millennium Falcon* will be Luke's next challenge. The dorsal hatch used in the film does not appear on the LEGO model! Still, a Jedi always finds a way...

**CLOUD CITY**
A thriving city built on a delicate spire, high above the remote planet Bespin. Home to gas miners and residents looking to escape from the chaos of the rest of the galaxy.

PHEW! TAKE YOUR TIME, GUYS, I'VE ONLY BEEN HANGING ON FOR *AGES*...

**WEATHER VANE**
A fragile atmosphere-analysing antenna under Cloud City, high above the gas giant planet Bespin.

# UNCERTAIN FUTURE

Back with the rebel fleet, Luke and his friends have a new mission. Somewhere out there, a frozen Han Solo needs their help. As Lando and Chewbacca depart in the *Millennium Falcon* to find him, Luke, Leia and the droids watch them go and wonder what the future holds in store.

## A NEW EPISODE

 There are 17 LEGO sets depicting the vehicles and events from Episode V.

 After this scene, Luke's minifigure only appears wearing his black Jedi robes or Endor camouflage gear.

SO LONG, SUCKERS!

So off went Chewbacca and Lando to Tatooine in search of Captain Solo. I was quite relieved that I wouldn't have to go there myself!

THEY, UH, *ARE* COMING BACK, RIGHT?

**MEDICAL FRIGATE**
The EF76 Nebulon-B escort ship *Redemption*, converted by the Rebel Alliance into a mobile hospital vessel.

# EPISODE VI

## RETURN OF THE JEDI

*Luke has returned to Tatooine to rescue Han from Jabba the Hutt. Pew! Pew! Take that! Aaargh!*

*And if that wasn't exciting enough, the Empire has now begun work on a new Death Star! Yikes!*

**Bigger, rounder and deathier than ever, it's enough to make your narrator run away before the end of his senten.....**

# NEW STAR RISING

The second Death Star is almost complete. Larger and more powerful than the original, it will soon mean the end of all of the Empire's enemies, especially the pesky Rebel Alliance. Darth Vader has come aboard personally to make sure the battle station is ready on time. Even more frightening for the Imperial crew, the Emperor himself will soon be arriving.

## DEATH STAR II

An Ultimate Collector's Series model of the Death Star II was released in 2005 (set 10143), and just like the space station in the movie, it is left unfinished. It still contains 3,449 pieces, though!

THE EMPEROR'S COMING HERE??

WE'RE GOING TO NEED A LOT MORE GREY BRICKS.

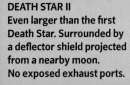

**THE OUTER RIM**
The largest and least explored part of known galaxy. The perfect location to construct a huge, top-secret, planet-destroying superweapon.

**DEATH STAR II**
Even larger than the first Death Star. Surrounded by a deflector shield projected from a nearby moon. No exposed exhaust ports.

**INCOMPLETE STRUCTU**
Someone should really
work on finishing the n
Death Star. It must be
pretty chilly in there.

**FOREST MOON OF ENDOR**
The furthest moon orbiting
the gas giant planet Endor.
Home to the Ewok species,
lots of trees and not much
else. Until now.

# JABBA THE HUTT

In Jabba the Hutt's palace on Tatooine, the large, slug-like crime lord has everything he wants: wealth, entertainment, all the slimy frogs he can eat and a frozen Han Solo hanging on his wall. Now he has something else, too: a masked bounty hunter has brought him Chewbacca the Wookiee.

## JABBA'S PALACE

 In 2003, an earlier version of Jabba's Palace was released as three sets, which could be fitted together.

 LEGO B'omarr monks, the former inhabitants of Jabba's palace, can be found in both Jabba's Palace sets.

**JABBA'S PALACE**
Former B'omarr monastery taken over by Jabba and his cronies. No one gets in or out without permission.

**FROZEN HAN SOLO**
There are just so many uses for a smuggler in carbonite. Wall hanging, end-table, backscratcher...

SORRY, OOLA, BUT YOU'VE BEEN VOTED OFF THE SHOW. TIME FOR THE NEXT CONTESTANT ON... HUTT IDOL!

**SALACIOUS B. CRUMB**
A Kowakian monkey-lizard, employed to make Jabba laugh.

"And there I was, Jabba the Hutt's new translator droid. Artoo claimed that it was part of some plan, but what did he know? We had clearly been abandoned to an awful fate indeed!"

**HO HO HO!**

**JABBA THE HUTT**
A powerful gangster who rules a large criminal empire. Gluttonous, greedy and unforgiving to his enemies. Not much nicer to his friends.

**CAPTURED WOOKIEE**
Chewbacca is not a fan of being shackled. He is also displeased to see Han Solo hung upon Jabba's wall.

**OOLA**
An unfortunate Twi'lek dancer who has just displeased the Hutt.

173

# THE BIG THAW

As Jabba and his court slumber, the bounty hunter known as Boushh creeps into Jabba's throne room and frees Han from his carbonite prison. Boushh removes her helmet – revealing herself to be none other than Princess Leia! But booming laughter interrupts their reunion… Jabba has seen everything. Now he has two more prisoners.

## HAN SOLO

 In the LEGO model, the trapped Han Solo is easily released by turning the carbonite piece around.

 Unlike most Han Solo minifigures, this version does not have a holster printed on his legs.

**LEIA'S DISGUISE**
To get inside Jabba's palace, Leia pretends to be the Ubese bounty hunter Boushh.

**BIB FORTUNA**
Jabba the Hutt's Twi'lek second in command. Like most of Jabba's staff, he isn't very trustworthy.

I THINK THAT CAN BE ARRANGED.

I'M STILL KINDA SLEEPY. CAN I GO BACK IN THE CARBONITE FOR THREE MORE HOURS?

**HIBERNATION SICKNESS**
After being thawed from the carbonite block, Han is still a little shaky… and temporarily blind from the deep freeze.

**HUTT CASTLE**
Headquarters of notorious crime lord Jabba the Hutt.

66 The very thought of the muculent crime lord known as Jabba the Hutt makes me feel as though I may malfunction. Having translated his rotten language, I can tell you that Jabba has no respect for droids. Or anyone else for that matter. 99

**MAX REBO**
Ortolan leader of the Max Rebo Band, under exclusive contract to Jabba. Plays the Red Ball Jett organ.

HO, HO! NEWPA POODOO.*

*TRANSLATION: HO, HO! NEW BANTHA FODDER!

HEHEHE! GOOD ONE, JABBA!

# RANCOR PIT

Now dressed in Jedi robes, Luke Skywalker comes to bargain for his friends' freedom. Instead of listening, Jabba tries to feed Luke to his ravenous pet rancor. When Luke escapes the creature's taloned clutches, Jabba is furious. He sentences Luke, Han and Chewie to be dropped into the Great Pit of Carkoon.

## RANCOR

The bone Luke uses to prop open the rancor's mouth does not actually fit into the LEGO rancor model. Unfortunately for the Gamorrean Guard, however, the rancor's mouth is big enough to fit a minifigure!

**MALAKILI**
Employed by Jabba to care for and train the rancor. Possibly the only being in the galaxy who doesn't hate rancors.

YIKES! WELL, HE DOES LOOK TASTY.

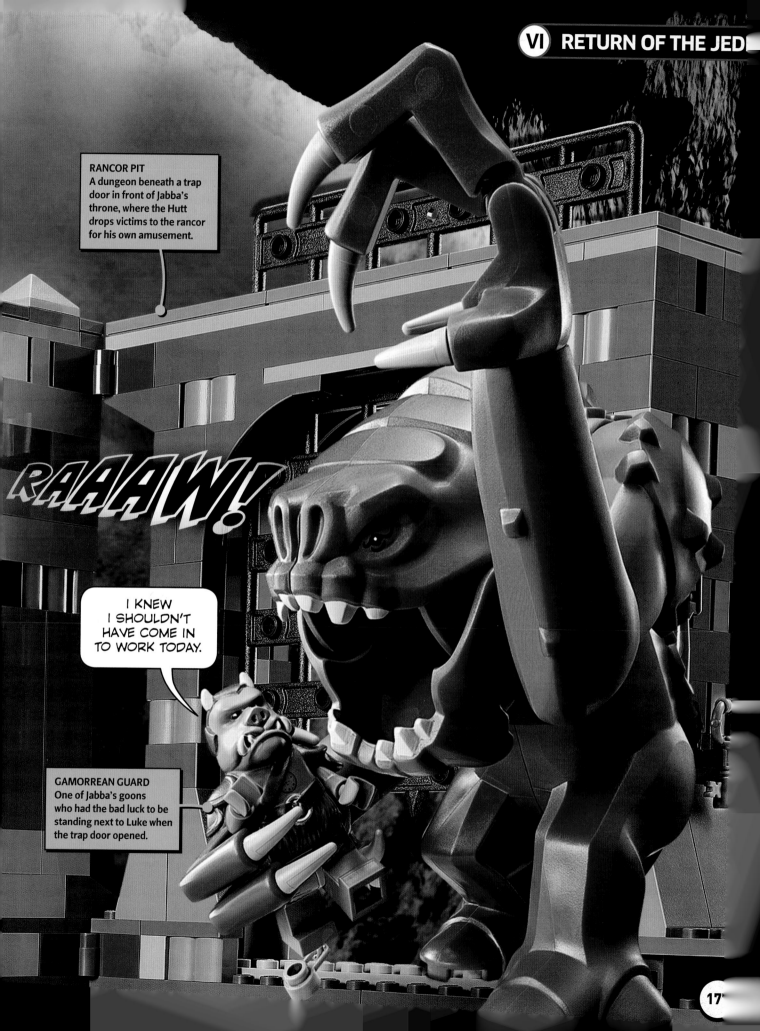

# A DARING ESCAPE

Jabba's prisoners are transported by desert skiff across the sand dunes to meet their fate at the hands of the man-eating Sarlacc. With Princess Leia chained to his side, Jabba watches the fun from his sail barge. But the gangster doesn't realise that this is all part of the heroes' plan. With Lando and R2-D2's help, Luke breaks free.

## DESERT SKIFF

 Incredibly, Han and Luke were left unguarded in the 2000 Desert Skiff set. They were the only two minifigures in the set!

 The latest version of the Sarlacc can fit two minifigures in its maw.

> PSST, LUKE! IT'S ME, LANDO!

**DISGUISED LANDO**
Posing as one of Jabba's guards, Lando is ready to lend assistance when the moment comes.

**DESERT SKIFF**
An open-topped repulsorlift cargo skiff used by Jabba to transport victims to the Pit of Carkoon.

> " And now everybody had been captured by Jabba! This plan that Artoo kept talking about seemed worse and worse. Jabba had him carrying drinks on the sail barge when he rushed off and launched something to Master Luke. It was his lightsaber! "

**LUKE'S LIGHTSABER**
Having lost his father's old lightsaber on Cloud City, Luke has built a new green-bladed one for himself.

**BOBA FETT**
The bounty hunter is still hanging around, enjoying being in Jabba's good books.

I KNOW IT'S YOU! HELP ME OUT, ALREADY!

**GREAT PIT OF CARKOON**
A sinkhole in the Northern Dune Sea of Tatooine inhabited by an enormous Sarlacc.

# THE LAST BOUNTY

All of Jabba's henchmen rush to stop the rebels from escaping. Leia deals with Jabba the Hutt, while chaos erupts on the deck of his sail barge. Even Boba Fett joins in the fight – but an accidental blow from the hibernation-blind Han Solo sends him hurtling into the pit. It is time to go.

**JABBA'S SAIL BARGE**
The *Khetanna*, a three-deck Ubrikkian Industries luxury sail barge. Its orange sails help with propulsion and shade passengers from Tatooine's suns.

**SARLACC**
A plant-like monster that lives under the sand and eats anything that falls into its toothy, beaked maw. Whatever ends up inside is slowly digested over the course of a thousand years.

# FINAL MOMENTS

Back on Dagobah, wise Yoda has finally reached the end of his days. Telling Luke that he must face Darth Vader in order to complete his training, the 900-year-old Jedi Master fades away. Before Luke leaves, the spirit of Obi-Wan Kenobi tells him one last secret. Luke has a twin sister – Leia.

## HIDEOUT
Yoda chose his Dagobah hideout with care. The planet was one of 37 planets erased from the Jedi Archives, making it almost impossible for the Empire to find him.

## LITTLE GREEN MAN

 Yoda's minifigure was the first ever to be released with short, non-poseable LEGO legs.

 Yoda lived for 900 years, but his minifigure is much younger: it was first released in 2002.

> YOU MUST CONFRONT VADER. ONLY THEN A JEDI WILL YOU BE.

## A LONG LIFE
Yoda has never revealed his home planet or his species, but a long life span appears to be a defining feature.

❝Master Yoda was a great Jedi. A wise teacher, a fierce general and a caring leader. Thank the Maker that he is able to live on in the Force – I can't imagine the chaos that would ensue otherwise!❞

WAIT, I ALREADY DID THAT. WOO-HOO! I'M A JEDI!

**JEDI OUTFIT**
He may not be a full Jedi Knight yet, but Luke is already starting to dress the part. Like Anakin before him, he favours black.

183

# THE REBEL BRIEFING

The Rebel Alliance is preparing for its greatest battle. Having learned of the new Death Star, they must act before it is completed. While the rebel fleet gathers for the attack, a commando team is sent to shut down the battle station's deflector shield generator on the sanctuary moon of Endor.

*HOME ONE*
A Mon Calamari-built star cruiser that serves as the rebels' command ship.

BEEP

IT'S A TRAP!!

ADMIRAL ACKBAR
Mon Calamari military commander of the Alliance Fleet.

GENERAL MADINE
One-time Imperial officer and planner of the commando strike on the shield generator.

**REBEL ALLIANCE**

*Home One* (set 7754) is the only set to include Mon Mothma and General Madine's minifigures.

Mon Mothma's hairstyle might look familiar – it is also sported by the Clone Wars version of Anakin!

" Captain Solo took the Endor mission, while Lando offered to lead the attack on the Death Star. Somehow, Artoo and I ended up on the commando force as well. Funny, I don't remember volunteering. "

BEEP

YOU DON'T EVEN KNOW WHAT THE PLAN IS YET, ACKBAR...

**MON MOTHMA**
Former Republic senator and one of the founders of the Rebel Alliance.

**LANDO CALRISSIAN**
Rebel Alliance General. Will pilot the *Millennium Falcon* during the battle.

BEEP

# STEALTH MISSION

Flying a stolen Imperial shuttle, Han, Luke, Leia, Chewie and the droids head towards Endor. They make it past the Empire's ships, but Darth Vader senses Luke's presence on board. The rebels land on the forest moon and begin their important mission.

**TYDIRIUM**
A *Lambda*-class T-4a Imperial shuttle captured by the Rebel Alliance. Its security codes are old, but still work. Probably.

WHAT'S THE SECRET PASSWORD?

"DARTH VADER SMELLS".

YOU MAY PASS.

**ENDOR**
The moon of Endor, orbiting the gas planet Endor in the Endor system. Small, but rich in plant and animal life.

## IMPERIAL SHUTTLE

 Seven LEGO models of the Imperial Shuttle have been released.

 The Ultimate Collector's Series Imperial Shuttle (10212) has space for four minifigures in the cockpit, but only one minifigure in the back.

# SPEEDER BIKE CHASE

As the rebel strike team makes its way through the forest, they are spotted by Imperial scout troopers on speeder bikes. Luke and Leia hop on a bike themselves and chase the scout troopers through an obstacle course of trees. It doesn't take long before the scout troopers are outmanoeuvred by the rebel heroes – but Leia gets lost along the way...

WHERE ARE THE BRAKES? WHERE ARE THE BRAKES??

**SCOUT TROOPER**
Imperial stormtroopers with lightweight armour for stealth and reconnaissance operations.

**SPEEDER BIKE**
74-Z repulsorlift speeder. Driving one requires extraordinarily quick reflexes and reaction times.

# VILLAGE IN THE TREES

Another danger, in addition to the Imperials, is the locals. A hidden net soon has the team trussed up and carried to the treetop village of the fuzzy but fierce Ewoks. There they find the missing Princess Leia... and also discover that the rest of them are about to be the main course at a feast.

I THINK THEY'VE MADE ME THEIR QUEEN! SO WHAT ARE YOU GUYS HERE FOR?

**EWOKS**
A tribe of short, fuzzy creatures from the forest moon of Endor. Not too fond of trespassers, even tasty ones.

YUB NUB!

## EWOK VILLAGE

The Ewok Village set holds various secrets, including tree trunk hiding places and a swinging spider's web!

One of the Ewoks seems to have a crush on Leia. Her name is inscribed inside a love heart on a LEGO tree.

EWOK VILLAGE
Known as Bright Tree
Village in the Ewok
language. A cluster of
huts and platforms built
in the treetops out of
logs, leaves and other
forest materials.

DINNER.

CATAPULT
Original Ewok design.
Built from all-natural
components – but no
less deadly for it.

# AHH... THE GOLDEN ONE

The Ewoks have big appetites, but the heroes have a Jedi on their side. Already convinced that the golden C-3PO is a mighty supernatural being, the Ewoks are most alarmed when the astonished protocol droid rises up into the air. With a little storytelling – complete with sound effects – the tribe is convinced to join the rebel cause.

## EWOKS

 There are seven Ewok minifigures. All have names, apart from one who is just known as Ewok Warrior.

 The facial hair on Wicket's minifigure has changed a lot over time. It used to be all dark brown.

**WICKET**
Wicket W. Warrick, a courageous young warrior and scout.

"TALK TO THE MOISTURE VAPORATOR, THREEPIO." "GO STAND QUIETLY IN THE CORNER, THREEPIO." "DO THIS, DO THAT, THREEPIO."

WELL, WHO'S GIVING THE ORDERS NOW? ME, THAT'S WHO! AH-HA-HA-HA!

**SEAT OF POWER**
A makeshift throne constructed by the Ewoks to carry their metal-plated deity.

192

This is my favourite part of the entire story! Me, the hero of the rebellion! Of course, I never doubted it myself, but it was nice to see the others acknowledge my vital role as well.

CHIEF CHIRPA
The leader of the Ewok tribe.

TEEBO
Ewok warrior. Wears a headdress made from the skull of an unfortunate gurreck beast.

LOGRAY
Head shaman. Interprets the "Golden One's" divine commands for the rest of the tribe.

YUB NUB?

193

# BUNKER SURPRISE

Having told Leia that he is her brother, Luke knows that he has to meet his father face-to-face and convince him to return to the light side of the Force. Meanwhile, the others infiltrate the bunker that houses the shield generator. But a large Imperial force sneaks up on them. Their mission has failed.

**FOREST MOON**
Forests here are made up of large pine and redwood trees.

FREEZE, YOU REBEL SCUM!

**IMPERIAL NAVY TROOPER**
Dressed in distinctive black helmet and uniform.

## SHIELD BUNKER

The doors of the authentically detailed bunker (set 8038) slide open with the turn of a cog.

In the movie, an entire legion of scout troopers retake the bunker. But in set 8038, there are just two!

> **"** Imperial troopers! They aren't the cleverest of adversaries, but they did manage to capture us and keep us from completing our mission. Thank goodness I didn't panic. **"**

THERE ISN'T ANY CHANCE YOU'LL JUST LET US BLOW THIS PLACE UP, RIGHT?

**REBEL COMMANDO**
A member of the rebel strike team sent to destroy the shield generator. Forest camouflage isn't so useful inside the bunker.

**POWER GENERATOR**
These electrified cones provide the deflector shield with its power.

# IT'S A TRAP

The rebel ships emerge from hyperspace, ready to attack the new Death Star, but its deflector shield is still up – there is nothing that they can do to damage it! Even worse, the entire Imperial fleet is waiting for them... and the Death Star's devastating superlaser isn't incomplete. It is fully armed and operational.

**B-WING FIGHTER**
A rebel starfighter and bomber with a gyro-stabilised rotating cockpit and mid-body S-foils.

**A-WING FIGHTER**
RZ-1 A-wing, the Rebel Alliance's fastest starfighter.

ACKBAR WAS RIGHT – IT IS A TRAP!

**SUPERLASER**
The ultimate weapon's ultimate weapon. Settings range from "powerful enough to obliterate a planet" to "delicate enough to blow up a rebel capital ship".

# A-WING

In the movie, a rebel A-wing pilot called Arvel Crynyd destroys Vader's flagship, the *Executor*. The 2013 LEGO A-wing model (set 75003) is piloted by an unnamed minifigure who strongly resembles Crynyd.

**TIE INTERCEPTOR**
Dagger-winged TIE fighter variation with improved speed and firepower.

# FATHER AND SON

In his throne room on the Death Star, Emperor Palpatine gloats in triumph. The rebels will soon be no more, and Darth Vader has brought him Luke Skywalker, his soon-to-be apprentice. Palpatine smiles as Vader and Luke lock lightsabers, knowing that whoever loses, the dark side will surely win.

## THRONE ROOM

 In the movie, Emperor Palpatine's throne room looks out onto a majestic view of space. His view in 2008's Death Star set (10188) is significantly less epic – he overlooks the hangar bay!

YOU DON'T KNOW THE POWER OF THE DARK SIDE, LUKE.

I KNOW IT REALLY MESSES UP FACES. LOOK AT YOU GUYS!

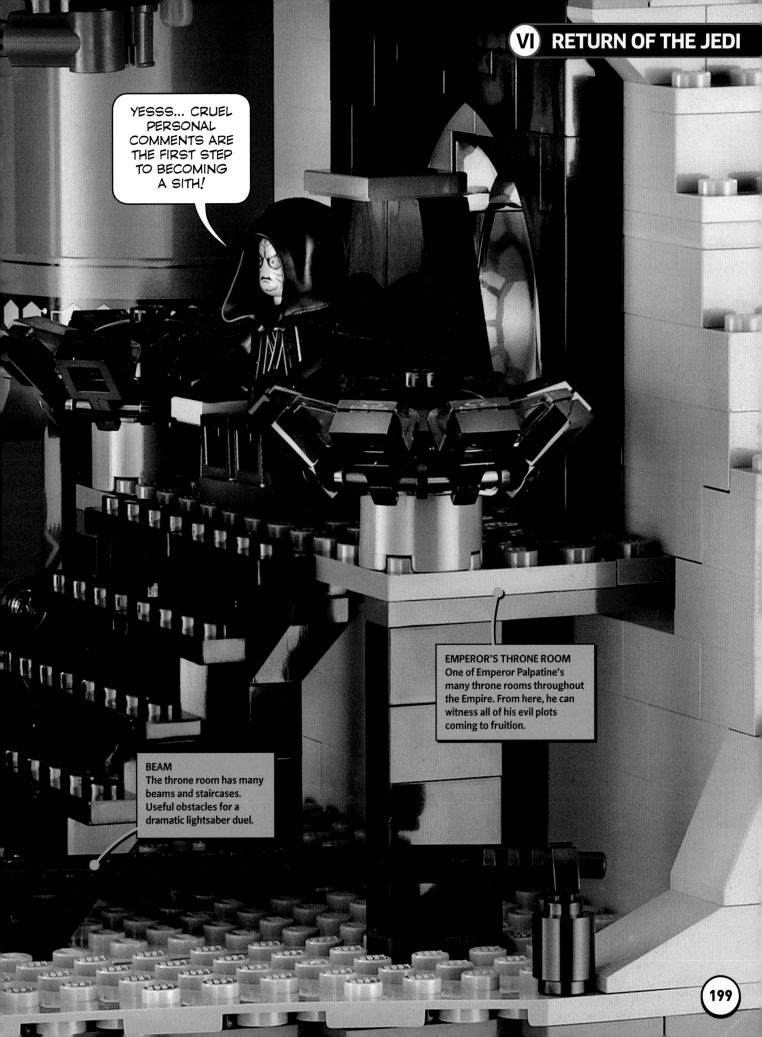

YESSS... CRUEL PERSONAL COMMENTS ARE THE FIRST STEP TO BECOMING A SITH!

**EMPEROR'S THRONE ROOM**
One of Emperor Palpatine's many throne rooms throughout the Empire. From here, he can witness all of his evil plots coming to fruition.

**BEAM**
The throne room has many beams and staircases. Useful obstacles for a dramatic lightsaber duel.

# THE BATTLE OF ENDOR

The Emperor's scheme to wipe out the rebellion is perfect in every way but one: he fails to anticipate the courage of a tribe of Ewok warriors. Coming to the aid of their new rebel friends with rocks, trees and hang gliders, the Ewoks battle the Imperial troopers and smash their armoured walkers to bits.

## AT-ST WALKERS

 Of the three minifigure-scale AT-STs released, only one comes with an AT-ST driver. The others are driven by Chewbacca!

 The AT-ST in the Battle of Endor set (8038) has a walking function.

**SHIELD GENERATOR BUNKER**
Secret entrance to the deflector shield generator complex. Has multiple strong and sturdy blast doors.

**ROCKS**
Ewok weapon of choice. Ubiquitous on the moon of Endor, and capable of destroying Imperial machinery if deployed effectively.

YUB NUB!

SOMEDAY I'M GOING TO FIND OUT WHAT "YUB NUB" MEANS.

❝ Artoo and I led the attack! Well, really we pretended that we were surrendering and lured the stormtrooper guards into an Ewok ambush. But those are basically the same thing, right? ❞

**EWOK HANG GLIDER**
Assembled out of sticks and hides. Actually works pretty well, amazingly enough.

YUB NUB!

YUB NUB!

**AT-ST**
All Terrain Scout Transport, the AT-AT's smaller, two-legged cousin. Seats two Imperial drivers, or one Wookiee and a pair of Ewoks.

# THE SHIELD IS DOWN!

Chewbacca and the Ewoks free the captured rebels, and they all get to work setting up explosives inside the bunker. The bunker and shield generator are obliterated in a massive blast. Up in space, the Death Star is suddenly open to attack. Lando, piloting the *Millennium Falcon*, is ready to lead the remaining rebel starfighters into the Death Star.

YUB NUB!

WE DID IT!

OOOARRGH!*
*TRANSLATION:
RUN!

# WRATH OF THE SITH

Luke has beaten Darth Vader in the duel, but the young man refuses to give in to anger and revenge. He casts aside his lightsaber and declares himself now and for evermore a Jedi. The Emperor is furious. He raises his hands and unleashes the full power of the dark side upon Luke.

**VIEWPORT**
A transparisteel window lets Palpatine view the crushing of the Rebel Alliance outside. If he takes a look at the moment, he'll be in for a surprise.

OOH, THAT TICKLES! WAIT... NO... ACTUALLY, IT FEELS TERRIBLE.

## THE EMPEROR

The Emperor's minifigure has had head pieces in yellow, grey and tan.

The Emperor favours the Force as a weapon. His minifigure brandishes LEGO Force lightning pieces more often than his lightsaber.

66 Poor, brave Master Luke. Down on Endor, I was unaware of his near sacrifice on board the Death Star. To think Emperor Palpatine – who, I'm told, was so kind back in his Chancellor days – could do such a thing! 99

*BZZT!* FORCE LIGHTNING IS THE COOLEST!!

**SITH STYLE**
Many Sith choose to wear a hooded cowl – it projects a certain menace.

*BZZZZT!*

ZZZZZ

WELL, WHADDYA KNOW. HE BROUGHT BALANCE TO THE FORCE AFTER ALL.

# EMPEROR NO MORE

Darth Vader can't stand to see the Emperor hurting his son. He has served the dark side for many long years, but he will serve it no longer. Picking up his former Master, he ignores the Force lightning crackling all around him and throws Darth Sidious down into the Death Star's deep reactor shaft.

## END OF THE SITH

▶ None of Palpatine's head pieces are printed with an expression of terror. Until now it hasn't been necessary.

▶ Perhaps the Emperor should speak to Darth Maul's minifigure about surviving such a long fall.

CRACKLE!

**REACTOR SHAFT**
An 80 km (50 mile) drop straight into the Death Star's power core. That's it for Emperor Palpatine.

# THE JEDI RETURNS

Mortally wounded by the Emperor's lightning, Darth Vader asks Luke to remove his mask. Luke does, at last looking upon the scarred face of Anakin Skywalker. Anakin tells Luke that he was right – there really had been good inside Darth Vader all along.

**SCARRED FACE**
Battle-damaged from past duels and Imperial missions, Anakin's face is totally unrecognisable to those who knew him in his Jedi days.

**EVACUATION**
As chaos reigns, stormtroopers and Death Star officers race to escape the damaged battle station.

BE HONEST, SON. HOW DO I LOOK?

**ANAKIN REDEEMED**
Although his life-support armour is too badly damaged to keep working, with his act of fatherly love and self-sacrifice, Anakin has brought himself back to the light side of the Force.

**BEHIND THE MASK**

Vader has been redeemed, but his good looks have not returned. His head piece is still grey and scarred.

Under Vader's LEGO helmet have been 12 different grey heads, two tan heads and one plain black head.

**IMPERIAL SHUTTLE**
Darth Vader's *Lambda*-class T4a shuttle. About to become Luke's getaway vehicle.

ER... GREAT, DAD! REALLY GREAT.

THIS IS NO TIME FOR A CATCH-UP... RUN!

# THE STAR EXPLODES

Lando flies the *Falcon* into the Death Star's core, accompanied by a lone X-wing. As the main reactor comes into sight, both ships fire. Racing ahead of the chain reaction they've just set off, they make it out of the battle station just in time. The Death Star's explosion can be seen in the sky from the moon of Endor below.

**DEATH STAR CORE**
Powered by the annihilation of tachyonic hypermatter. Destroyed by concussion missiles. A detonating Sith Master may have contributed, too.

**WEDGE ANTILLES**
Although his name may not be as famous as Luke Skywalker's or Han Solo's, Wedge has been a key part of every major battle against the Empire.

66 Having been instrumental in destroying the Death Star's shield generator, I was pleased to see the huge explosion in the skies above Endor. Not to mention relieved that my dangerous life of adventure was surely over now. 99

THOOOM!

WOW, WE SURVIVED!

AW, THAT MEANS I HAVE TO GIVE HAN HIS SHIP BACK...

*MILLENNIUM FALCON*
The *Falcon* used to belong to Lando Calrissian, before Han Solo won it from him in a game of sabacc. Lando is happy to pilot it once more.

## REBEL HEROES

Lando Calrissian appears in four LEGO sets, none of which feature the *Falcon*. Twice he wears a cape and twice his skiff guard disguise.

Despite his heroics, Wedge Antilles appears in just one LEGO set (6212).

# FORCE FRIENDS

The victorious rebel fleet returns to Endor in triumph, and a few old friends drop by to watch the festivities. The Force spirits of Anakin, Obi-Wan and Yoda proudly look on as Luke, the last remaining Jedi, reunites with his friends.

**GALACTIC PEACE**
On thousands of planets across the galaxy, Imperial rule is no more. Peace and freedom can once again be enjoyed by all.

WELL DONE, LUKE, THE GALAXY IS FREE THANKS TO YOU.

YES, PROUD OF YOU, WE ARE.

**JEDI UNITED**
Anakin, Obi-Wan and Yoda are united in the Force.

## OLD FRIENDS

Although there are LEGO bricks that depict hologram minifigures, there are no LEGO Force spirits yet.

Luke has had many chances to make lots of LEGO friends – his minifigure appears in 30 sets!

THANKS GUYS... BUT I HEARD THERE WAS A PARTY GOING ON. THIS ISN'T IT... IS IT?

# A FREE GALAXY

While newly free worlds all over the galaxy celebrate the end of the Empire, the heroes join together for a joyous victory party on Endor. The Ewoks dance and sing all through the night, and Luke, Leia, Han and Chewie wonder what the future has in store...

## NOT QUITE THE END

LEGO® *Star Wars*™ is the longest running of any licensed LEGO theme. 2014 was its 15th anniversary.

In total, there are 434 LEGO *Star Wars* sets and an incredible 127 minifigures (so far)!

I WONDER WHAT WILL HAPPEN NEXT...

GUESS WE'LL FIND OUT IN EPISODE VII!

FIREWORKS
A combination of festive pyrotechnics released by rebel starfighters and fragments of the Death Star igniting in the atmosphere of Endor.

" And so our adventure came to a close, at least for the moment. But as we all know, it's a big galaxy, so there will always be new battles to fight, alliances to make and villains to overcome. In fact, I believe you could say that the story was just beginning! "

YUB NUB!!

BE-DWEEEEP!

THERE'S GOING TO BE AN EPISODE VII? WHY DIDN'T ANYONE TELL ME?

CELEBRATIONS
The Ewoks are skilled warriors, but they also insist on celebrating happy times with tribal dancing. New members of the tribe are invited to join in.

215

# INDEX

**"** Beep beeeeep! Blorp bop. Be-deeep. Beep bleep! Boop beee-doop. De-beep bleeeeep! Breeet be-doop. Be-deeep! Blorp boop beep! **"**